Introduction to
Software Defined
Networking —

Openflow & VxLAN

Vishal Shukla

ISBN-10: 1482678136

ISBN-13: 9781482678130

Library of Congress Control Number: 2013904616

CreateSpace Independent Publishing Platform

North Charleston, SC

Preface

Technologies always evolve to have better, simpler, and less expensive solutions to the problems of that time period. In the post-web 2.0 era, where the data traffic has increased many times over and more than fifty percent of Internet traffic is time-critical video streaming, the need for a newly designed network was imminent. Networks have evolved to keep pace with data traffic needs (From circuit/packet switching, to complex networking protocols running on one hundred–gigabyte network speed), the next step is software-defined networks (SDN).

For the past couple of years, there have been a lot of studies and research on how a network can follow the evolution of server virtualization. The trend began to form when companies started investing serious money into research and development of SDN. The precise definition of SDN is still evolving, but the general principle and fundamental protocols have been put in place to give it a direction.

This book is written to explain SDN for educational purposes. It focuses on one of the most promising protocols of SDN: OpenFlow. This book also touches on other SDN implementation, mainly VxLAN.

This book is based on the OpenFlow spec 1.0.0 and first draft of VxLAN, and I encourage readers to e-mail input and observations to us for the next edition: sdnbook@outlook.com.

Contents

Acknowledgments

Thanks to my friends, who helped me review this book multiple times; without their help, it would not have been possible. I want to thank Ashish Kapur for helping me in forming the chapter for VxLAN and Thu Tran for giving valuable inputs for OpenFLow Chapters. A big thanks to my wife Nandini, son Vinayak & my extended family back in India, who helped me to write this book by excusing my absence while working on the manuscript.

I dedicate this book to my parents, Kusum Shukla & the late P.N. Shukla, who are always a source of inspiration and guidance for me.

Chapter One
Introduction to SDN

1.1 Software-Defined Networks

With the explosive growth of data traffic over the past few years, the bottlenecks of traditional data networks have been exposed. An emerging technology, software-defined networking is an attempt to solve the bottlenecks of traditional switching/routing-based networking deployments. SDN uses the following three principles:

► Separation of control-plane functionality from switching *Application Specific Integrated Circuit* ASICs (by taking control-plane functionality to controller) and using the switching ASIC for data-plane functionalities only (hence, commoditizing the switching ASIC and reducing the complexity of specialized ASICs)

► A centralized controller and central view of the deployed network (including networking devices and servers/virtual machines)—the idea here is to abstract the details of complex networking (which is based on complex routing/switching protocols and virtual machines)

► Extensibility by proving an open standard can program the network by simple external applications

There have been several implementations from different vendors, depending on how they view SDN. Some vendors are focusing on OpenFlow-based controllers, and some are working on developing the network from a virtual-machine point of view (abstracting the network switches), such as VxLAN-based solutions. Essentially, SDN is anything that satisfies the above three conditions.

In Figure 1.1, the left-hand side block represents the current network deployments typically having switches/routers interconnected to each other and devices (servers/Virtual Machines (VMs)) on the edge. The current network deployments rely on using the distributed protocols to build the control path. Once the control path is done, the data plane is installed on the hardware, and normal traffic passes on a programmed path. In current deployments, these control protocols are distributed across the network to make control and data paths that are mainly Layer-2 and Layer-3 protocols, like BGP, OSPF, and STP.

The right-hand side block in Figure 1.1 shows the SDN definition of the same network, wherein the Network Operating System (OS) will run at one single entity (e.g., controller), and all flow-based decisions will be made by this entity. Once the decision is taken, the controller will program the data plane of the switch, making the network. The dotted line in the right half of Figure 1.1 shows the communication between controller and networking devices. On these links, the controller can have the full view of deployments. The solid links are regular data links on which the data will flow once the switching/routing hardware is installed.

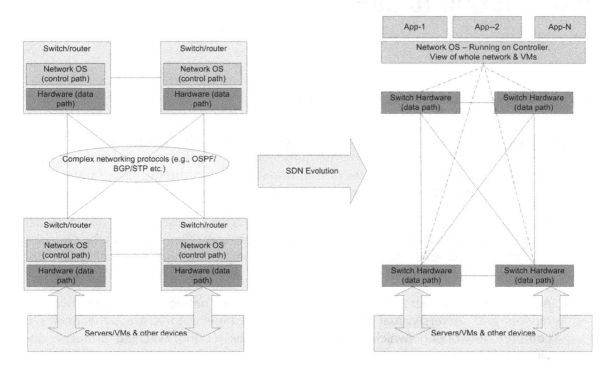

Figure 1.1

Segregation of Control Plane and Data Plane

The goal of SDN is to make sure that all control-level logical decisions are taken at a central place, as compared to traditional networking, wherein control-level decisions are taken locally and intelligence is distributed in each switch. Having this central approach will reduce the need for N number of intelligent nodes in an N-nodes topology.

SDN is based upon the fact that the hardware ASIC became a commodity, and there is no need to have specialized ASIC for making the networks—the real difference now is the software. The basic usage of any network software is to program the path so that the traffic can flow on that specific path. Now, with hardware being a commodity and software dependency on hardware diminishing, there is no need to have the intelligent software running on all nodes. SDN leverages this concept by running the software logic at a centralized place (e.g., the controller) and by programming the switches (commodity hardware) using southbound protocols/Application program interfaces (APIs).

SDN Controller

Central controller (SDN controller) is a software entity that is meant to have a global view of the entire network (including the VMs and traffic flows). As explained in Figure 1.1, the network operating system, which runs all logic for path selection, should run on this central SDN controller. Because the controller will have the view of the entire network, it can decide on the optimized flow and program the entries in the hardware. Currently most of the SDN controllers have a graphical-user interface, which can give a pictorial view of the entire network to the administrator.

Controllers are also viewed as platforms that can be used to run the applications to control the networks. These applications need not know the complex physical infrastructure beneath the controller. The typical examples of these applications are flow analysis or event-triggered programming of the network.

There can be more than one controller in the network, hence supporting the high availability of the control plane. Regular synchronization happens when there is more than one controller for a network.

Extensibility by Providing Programming of Networks

The abstraction of physical-network topology and deployment is one of the major benefits of SDN. However, the biggest charm of SDN is something else. The administrator can write applications that run on top of the OpenFlow controller, and the controller can talk to Open-Flow switches for installing the flows, thus, keeping the actual switch layer abstracted from the application layer. The APIs for writing these applications are provided by controllers (hooks in the controller code).

The example of this model is an administrator writing an application so that whenever the CEO of his or her company hosts a web conference it is given the highest priority. He or she can write a basic application with a simple trigger and leave everything to the controller, which will talk to the API written by the administrator and then translate it into control-plane flow definition, which supports this application action when triggered. The controller may tell networking HW devices to give maximum buffers which are coming from CEO multicast server, and all other flows get lower buffers).

Logical Layers of SDN

Figure 1.2 explains the three-tier logical layers of SDN. As explained in Figure 1.2, the lowest level is the switching hardware; the middle layer is the controller layer; and the top layer is the application layer in which a user can define the applications that will trigger the definition of flows in the network.

Southbound APIs

Southbound APIs/protocol are a set of APIs and protocols that work between the two bottommost layers (the switching ASIC or VMs) and the middle layer (the controller). Its main purpose is the communication that allows a controller to install control-plane decision on hardware, thus, controlling the data plane. OpenFlow is the most promising southbound protocol, which has enough hooks to control the network.

There are some more implementations being researched to explore other ways of implementing southbound communications. For example, VxLAN is one such standard that makes a detailed map of end servers/VMs and define that end stations map as network. It essentially assumes that switching networks (switches/routers) need not be programmed, and it abstracts that from view of the SDN controller. It defines SDN by controlling VMs and having the SDN controller define the domains and flows based on those VMs traffic, without programming the Ethernet switches (which it assumes can use any existing protocol to provide path on Ethernet fabric).

Eventually southbound APIs have to evolve, wherein it has end-to-end view of networks (including switching/routing devices and VMs/end nodes), and as such, an administrator can program networking devices (the switching ASICs) and the VMs with a single SDN controller.

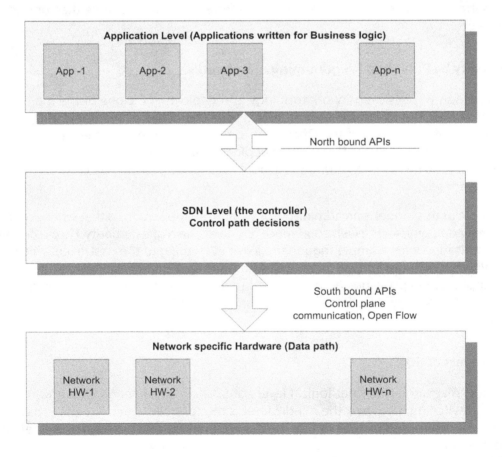

Figure 1.2

Northbound APIs

In between the middle and top layers, there will be API level of communication, wherein a user can define the application, and that application can communicate to the controller using northbound API, and the controller can translate it to flow to the lowest layer (e.g., switching hardware). As of now, there is not much traction in writing the northbound APIs, but with the increase in deployments of SDN, having many northbound APIs develop will be a natural, progressive path. For now, Quantum API is an open northbound API integrated with many OpenFlow/SDN controllers.

Enabling Technologies

To conclude, here are all the enabling technologies for SDN:

- ► Commodity (programmable) switches and servers/VMs

- ► Southbound protocols (OpenFlow protocol)

- ► SDN controller

- ► Northbound APIs

This book focuses mainly on OpenFlow technology, but it does cover VxLAN on a conceptual level.

1.2 What Is OpenFlow?

As explained in Section 1.1, OpenFlow is essentially a southbound protocol. Here is a more detailed explanation of OpenFlow.

- ► OpenFlow is an example of software-defined networking, and, as the name suggests, the networking between two end points is defined through the software running on an external PC/server, and the actions are programmed on hardware (switches) based on the intelligent decisions taken by the controller.

- ► OpenFlow is an open, standards-based protocol that defines how the control plane can be configured and controlled by a central place (the controller). By using OpenFlow, the controller can manage how data packets are forwarded through the network.

- ► In a traditional network, the switches and routers have information stored in different formats (routing table, Mac table, etc.) that are calculated by complex switching and routing protocols running on a whole or set of networks. Based on these tables, the data plane is programmed. OpenFlow protocol standardizes a single and centralized protocol that can create and manage the flow tables, replacing all other forwarding tables. The data plane is then programmed based on these flow tables.

OpenFlow Components

As shown in Figure 1.3, the main pieces of OpenFlow are: OpenFlow controller, OpenFlow switch, and OpenFlow protocol.

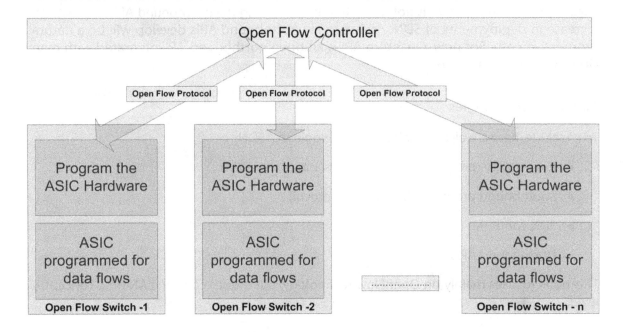

Figure 1.3

OpenFlow controller.

This is the brain of the protocol, making all intelligent decisions per flow and pushing those decisions to OpenFlow switches. These decisions stay in flow table in the form of actions. Typical per-flow decisions may be in the form of: adding, deleting, and modifying a flow in OpenFlow switch; configuring OpenFlow switch to contact controller for all unknown packets; and some actions on OpenFlow table.

The variables taken into account to define a flow are called tuples. As per the OpenFlow 1.0 spec, there are twelve variables on which the decisions can be taken.

OpenFlow switch.

On hardware level, OpenFlow switch is like a typical networking switch used in current networking. What is missing in it is the software intelligence. In OpenFlow switch, the OpenFlow controller manages hardware flow tables, and switch capabilities are mainly used for data-plane forwarding. The control path is taken care of by the OpenFlow controller, and the date path is made based on the ASIC programming done by the OpenFlow controller.

OpenFlow protocol.

OpenFlow protocol is similar to any typical networking protocol where in the end goal is to have the data path programmed. However, the approach to have the data path programmed is different in OpenFlow. OpenFlow is a fusion of client-server technology and various networking protocol. This book explains OpenFlow in detail by doing a deep dive in packets. Chapters Two to Five explain OpenFlow in detail.

1.3   Why OpenFlow?

Necessity is the mother of invention. To know why OpenFlow was invented, the current networking technologies' pitfalls need to be looked at from a critical perspective.

The current networking deployments are based on around 5,000 RFCs (Request for comments)—or hundreds of models of specialized hardware chip sets and so on. Here are the typical behavior and issues with current networking technologies that we have.

Current deployment of Networking devices in data centers	Issues associated with these current deployments.
In a typical network there are hundreds of switches/routers. Typically every rack in a data center has a top of rack switch.	All these needs to be Managed, Configured separately which is quite costly and complex job.
In a data center thousands of rack switches are configured using automated infrastructure. This is known as - automation of network. This is done using some type of scripting language.	This Automation procedure is highly complex procedure and comes with a huge price.
Intelligence is distributed among these hundreds of nodes. Each node is supposed to speak some kind of intelligent protocol (STP, BGP, OSPF etc.) – to communicate its uplink/downlink.	Distributed intelligence makes it difficult to manage and adds complexity in the user view of the deployment. The protocols between these nodes may not be same across the deployment which adds complexity on top.
Virtualization of Servers adds into more complex interaction on local network (more on access switch).	With more servers being virtualized, the access switches are getting more intelligent and hence the manageability of network is getting more complex.
Fixed set of features – dependent on Hardware and the software locally running on networking node.	This results in dependency on hardware and software to be changed at node level, if any design change is happening at deployment.
Flexibility of changing the flow as per user application is limited.	The flows are typically based on pre-defined tables and pre-defined protocols. Most of the protocols do not give enough knobs to users to change the flow as per design.

Table 1.1

In Table 1.1, the issues associated with the current network deployments are discussed line by line. Most of the issues can be resolved by using OpenFlow protocol:

- Having the controller taking all control-level decisions eliminates the need for intelligent switches, thus, reducing the huge cost of buying intelligent switching software.

- Since the switches will not need to be configured/managed separately, the cost incurred to automate the network will be less, Flat view of the network makes it simpler to manage.

- No dependency on complex routing/switching protocols.

With SDN concepts, a programmable network can be achieved, wherein an administrator can program the network based on the applications. This is a more direct approach for putting the pieces together instead of the discrete approach in current networks.

Chapter Two
Overview of Openflow

This chapter explains the OpenFlow protocol from a bird's-eye view. A very simple example is used to explain what happens when a packet comes in to an OpenFlow switch. This protocol typically works like client-server methodology, wherein a server (running controller software on it) programs the client (or the switch) to tell it how to handle the flows (or traffic). The easiest way to understand the OpenFlow operation is to go through each step of a basic-flow diagram. In this chapter, we will go through different steps of a simple OpenFlow-based flow diagram.

2.1   OpenFlow Protocol Overview

In the flow diagram of Figure 2.1, a letter indicates each major step, starting with A (Step 0 is the discovery stage). To make it a basic-flow diagram, the topology is assumed to be a single link between an OpenFlow client (switch) and OpenFlow controller (server). To start on Step 0, there should be connectivity between the OpenFlow switch (which is running in pure OpenFlow mode) and the OpenFlow controller.

Step 0

This is where the connection is established between the OpenFlow switch and OpenFlow controller. The connection between a controller and a single switch is made one to one (more than one OpenFlow switch can be reachable using management network). The connection between server and client is a TCP connection. The details on how this connection is formed are discussed in later sections.

Step A

This step explains when a packet comes to an OpenFlow switch if part of an OpenFlow network. In this flow diagram, the OpenFlow switch is assumed to be running in OpenFlow mode, and thus, when the packet comes to switch, it will be given to the OpenFlow client module running in switch. This incoming packet can be a control packet or a data packet.

Step B

In this step, the switch takes care of (physical layer) PHY-level processing—this is vendor-specific implementation and depends on the type of link the OpenFlow switch has (fiber or copper). Once processed, the packet is given to the OpenFlow client running on the client switch.

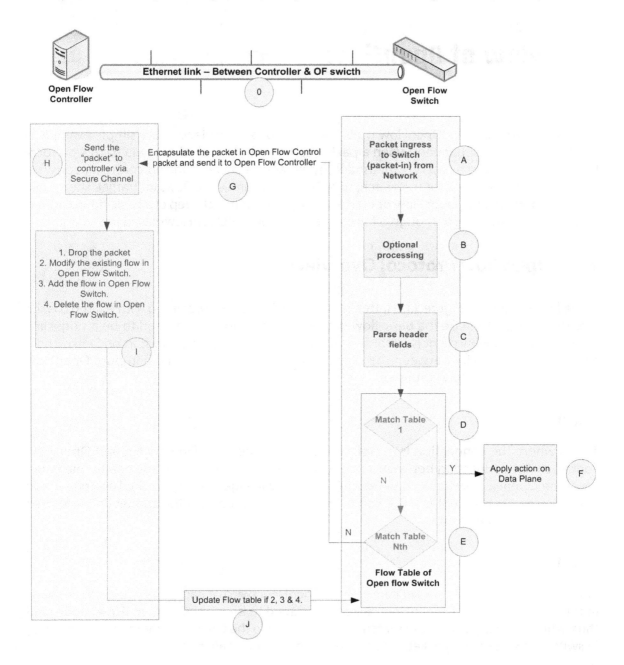

Figure 2.1 Flow diagram of OpenFlow protocol.

Step C

Once the packet is inside the switch for processing, the OpenFlow client running inside the switch analyzes the headers of the packet to understand what kind of packet it is. This is typically done to extract one of the twelve tuples inside the packet so that it can match it based on the flow tables installed in later steps.

Steps D and E

Once the switch has the tuple information on what can be matched, it starts scanning the flow table, starting from Flow 1 to Flow N. Once the list is scanned, the action listed in that flow is taken (this is explained in more detail in the next section). Different implementations can be done to optimize the scanning and make the flow table more efficient so that less scans are done.

Step F

If the tuple is matched, the action associated with that specific flow is done. Typically the action is to forward the packet, drop the packet, or send it to the controller. If the action is to forward the packet from the switch, the packet will be switched. If there is no action listed for a flow, then it is an implicit drop for that flow (as such, the packet will be dropped). If there are no flow-entry matches to that packet, it will be sent to the controller (after encapsulating it in a OpenFlow control packet).

Steps G and H

If the tuples extracted from the ingress packet do not match with any of the entry-in-flow table, then the packet is encapsulated in packet-in header and sent to the controller for further action. As per the protocol, the controller needs to decide on what needs to be done with this new flow.

Note: Packet-in header is explained in further sections.

Step I

The controller looks at the packet and, based on the configurations done on the controller, decides what to do. The typical decision would be to drop the packet (do nothing about it), install/modify the flow table on OpenFlow switches (with an action specified with it), or consume it to modify configurations on the controller itself.

Step J

If the controller decides to add/modify the flow table on the switch, then it sends a relevant control message to the OpenFlow switch.

Once the flow is installed, the next packet coming from the flow table will be taken care of per Step F. For every new flow, these steps would be repeated. The flows can be deleted based on the implementation on the OpenFlow switch and OpenFlow controller.

2.2 Overview of OpenFlow Components

2.2.1 OpenFlow Controller

The OpenFlow controller is the core of any OpenFlow-based software-defined network. This is a software that runs the control plane and programs the flows on network switches based on the control plane logics (for example, the shortest paths are calculated into the controller and then programmed on the switches). The controller runs on a powerful server, which should be reachable by all OpenFlow switches. For ease of usability, the controls are provided to the administrator/user via a powerful GUI with many knobs to control the networks.

The OpenFlow switches reach out for the controller if any new event not listed in the flow table occurs. Current controllers available on the market have the ability to give an entire network view on the GUI. Many of them can pictorially represent the flows going in that network.

The other major evolving segment in SDN is the applications that a network administrator can write on SDN controllers. Current controllers provide the APIs, which can be used to develop the applications that can run on the controller and customize the logic of the control plane. By writing applications on controllers, the network administrators can control the flows.

2.2.2 OpenFlow Switch

OpenFlow switch is a typical networking switch that lacks the intelligent protocols on it. OpenFlow switch will run the software-required bare minimum to connect to the OpenFlow controller and install and analyze flows. At this stage, the definition of OpenFlow switch is vendor specific. On high level, OpenFlow switch can be classified in two categories:

1. Pure OpenFlow Switch: This switch supports only OpenFlow protocol.

2. Hybrid OpenFlow Switch: This switch supports traditional Ethernet protocols in addition to networking protocols.

Regardless of switch type, an OpenFlow switch will support a module to make a connection (SSH/TCP) with the OpenFlow controller and a flow table, which is configured by the OpenFlow controller based on the controller implementation.

2.2.3 Flow Table

Flow table resides in OpenFlow switch, and it tells the switch how to handle any flow coming to that particular switch. The OpenFlow controller populates the flow table in an OpenFlow switch and based on various flows and the physical topology view of the controller.

All incoming traffic in OpenFlow switch is processed based on this flow table. If there is no entry for a particular flow in the flow table, the flow information goes to the controller so that a decision on what to do with that new flow coming to the switch can be made. Once the controller decides on how to process the new flow, it programs that flow in OpenFlow switch, with relevant action.

Figure 2.2 summarizes how a flow table and a flow-match process look in an OpenFlow switch.

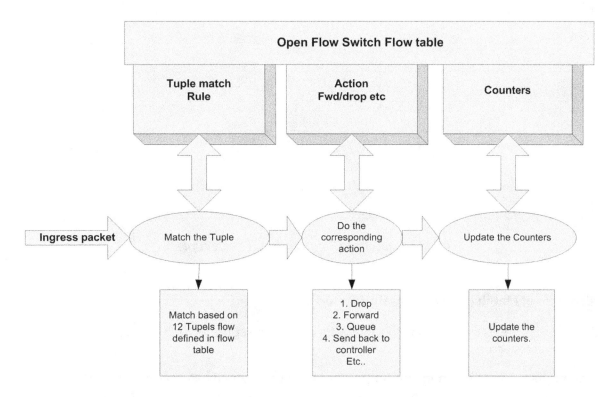

Figure 2.2

Each flow-table entry includes:

- Header fields to match incoming packets/flows (typically known as tuples)
- Counters to update for matching packet/bytes per flow
- Actions that should be taken if a flow is matched

Flow Table Header Fields (Tuples)

Any incoming packet in the switch needs to match a specific value (or a wild mask based matching) out of these twelve tuples of the header field. Most of these tuples are vendor specific as of now.

Field	bits	When applicable	Details
Ingress Port	16	All packets	Numerical Representation of incoming port
Ethernet Source address	48	All packets	L2 MAC source address
Ethernet destination address	48	All packets	L2 MAC destination address
Ether Type	16	All packets on enabled ports	An OpenFlow switch is required to match the type in both standard Ethernet and 802.2 with a SNAP header and OUI of 0x000000. The special value of 0x05FF is used to match all 802.3 packets without SNAP headers.
Vlan ID	Last 12	All packets of Ethernet type 0x8100	0xffff means untagged
Vlan Priority	Last 3	All packets of Ethernet type 0x8100	VLAN PCP field
IP Source Address	32	All IP and ARP packets	L3 Source IP address
IP Destination address	32	All IP and ARP packets	L3 Destination IP address
IP protocol	8	App IP and ARP packets	Only the lower 8 bits of ARP op-codes are used
IP TOS bits	First 6	All IP packets	Specify as 8-bit value and place TOS in upper 6 bits
TCP/UDP Source ports	16	All TCP, UDP and ICMP packets	Only lower 8 bits used for ICMP Type
TCP/UDP Destination ports	16	All TCP, UDP and ICMP packets	Only Lower 8 bits used for ICMP codes

Table 2.1 Details of flow headers (twelve tuples).

Example of Match (IPv4 Destination-Based Match)

Figure 2.3 is the example of a flow table with wild mask set for all tuples except destination IP address set to 10.1.1.1.

The figure shows that an incoming packet with Ether type 0x0800 and with destination IP 10.1.1.1 hits the switch, and as per OpenFlow protocol, it is then matched with respect to different entries of flow table. As per the flow table shown in the figure, all other fields are wild-card masked. The packet will look for a matching tuple.

If an incoming packet matches this flow entry, the action field of that flow will be based on the action that will be taken (if there is no action listed after flow is matched, it means it will be dropped). Default behavior is to encapsulate the packet and send a packet-in to the controller if the packet is not matched to any flow entry.

Once the action is decided, the counters are also updated. The counters can be used for a variety of purposes.

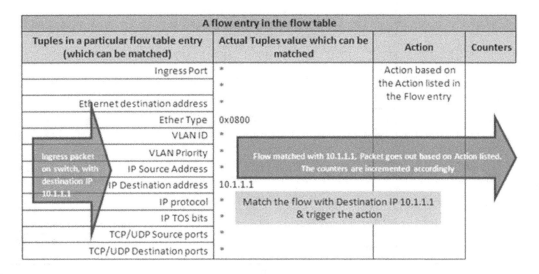

A flow entry in the flow table			
Tuples in a particular flow table entry (which can be matched)	Actual Tuples value which can be matched	Action	Counters
Ingress Port	*	Action based on the Action listed in the Flow entry	
	*		
Ethernet destination address	*		
Ether Type	0x0800		
VLAN ID	*		
VLAN Priority	*		
IP Source Address	*		
IP Destination address	10.1.1.1		
IP protocol	*		
IP TOS bits	*		
TCP/UDP Source ports	*		
TCP/UDP Destination ports	*		

Ingress packet on switch, with destination IP 10.1.1.1

Flow matched with 10.1.1.1. Packet goes out based on Action listed. The counters are incremented accordingly

Match the flow with Destination IP 10.1.1.1 & trigger the action

Figure 2.3

Counters

This is the second component of the flow table, and as per OpenFlow spec 1.0.0, it is maintained per flow, port, queue, and table. What counters will be implemented is also vendor specific. Counters are mainly used to send the statistical information to the controller.

Actions

This is the third component of the flow table, which specifies what action should be taken if a flow entry is matched with the incoming packet (as explained in Figure 2.3). Flow entry may be associated with zero or more actions. Based on the actions in the flow table, the switch processes the incoming packet. If there is no action associated with the flow, the switch will drop the packet. If there is more than one action attached to a flow entry, then the actions will be executed exactly in the order listed in the flow table. If a switch cannot perform the action or cannot perform it in the specific order as programmed by the controller, it will send an error message to the controller and will not program the flow.

Action – classification	Action	Applies on	Details
Required Action	Forward	Specific port	Forward the traffic to the specified known (Physical or Logically defined) port.
		ALL	Send the packet out all interfaces (physical or Logically defined), not including the incoming interface.
		Controller	Forward the packet to the controller. Encapsulate and send the packet to controller (do a packet-in)
		Local	Send the packet to the switches local networking stack (applies in case of Hybrid switch).
		Table	Perform actions in flow table, triggered by packet out event only. For example – Packet out from controller, to do a table look-up and do the action specified in the matched flow.
		In Port	Send the packet out the input (ingress) port.
	Drop		A flow-entry with no specified action indicates that all matching packets should be dropped.
Optional Action	Forward	Normal	Switch the packet using Normal Ethernet forwarding - i.e. using L2/L3 (Switches in hybrid mode supports this).
		Flood	Flood the packet on spanning tree links, not including the incoming port.
	Modify field		This action specifies the actions which can modify the packets/flow before doing any action (if there is more action). Explained in detail in table 2.4.
	Enqueue		The enqueue action forwards a packet through a queue attached to a port. Forwarding behavior is dictated by the configuration of the queue and is used to provide basic QOS per port.

Table 2.2 Summary of actions.

Here are the detailed definitions of action classifications shown in Table 2.2.

Action Classification

Based on the OpenFlow specification 1.0, the action is classified into two categories. As of now, per 1.0 specification, the OpenFlow switch needs to support only required actions.

Required action:

- Action of forwarding a packet to known physical ports or to virtual ports (Note: virtual ports are a set of ports with similar characteristics, for example: "local port" means ports local to switch)
- Action of dropping a packet if there is no action specified with a flow entry

Optional action:

- Action of forwarding a packet using legacy L2/L3 protocols—if a switch supports this functionality, it can forward the packet, using normal L2/L3 protocols (for example, VLAN forwarding)
- Action of modifying a field before any other action
- Enqueue a packet—the enqueue action specifies that a packet should go through the queue defined by the QOS on that port

Modify Field

This is an optional action in OpenFlow 1.0 specification. It makes the protocol flexible and gives better control on specific fields on flow. Table 2.3 has the summary of all operations that can be done when using the modify field as an action associated with a flow.

Action	Bits to be modified	Description
Set Vlan ID	12	This action specifies that a VLAN ID can be modified (adding a new ID or changing the ID). This modification can be used to translate VLANs and swap VLANs ID, hence providing a good solution to many problems.
Set VLAN Priority	3	This action specifies that a VLAN Priority can be modified (adding a VLAN priority or changing the Priority) . This modification can be used to modify priorities, hence providing a god solution to some specific use cases.
Strip VLAN header		Strip the VLAN header if present, and hence providing some flow level solution to some specific use cases.
Modify Ethernet Source MAC address	48	Replace the existing Ethernet source MAC address with the desired value. This can provide the better packet level control, to work with some specific use cases.
Modify Ethernet destination MAC address	48	Replace the existing Ethernet destination MAC address with the value with the desired value. This can provide the better packet level control, to work with some specific use cases.

Modify IPv4 Source address	32	Replace the existing IP source address with the new desired value and update the IP check sum (and TCP/UDP checksum if applicable). The action is only applicable to IPv4 packets. This can provide the better packet level control, to work with some specific use cases.
Modify IPv4 destination address	32	Replace the existing IP destination address with the new desired value and update the IP checksum (and TCP/ UDP checksum if applicable). This action is only applied to IPv4 packets. This can provide the better packet level control, to work with some specific use cases.
Modify IPv4 ToS bits	6	Replace the existing IP Tos fields with desired value. This action only applied to IPv4 packets. This can provide the better packet level control, to work with some specific use cases.
Modify transport source port	16	Replace the existing TCP/UDP source port with new desired value and update the TCP/UDP checksum. This action is only applicable to TCP and UDP packets. This can provide the better packet level control, to work with some specific use cases.
Modify transport destination	16	Replace the existing TCP/UDP destination port with the new desired value and update the TCP/UDP checksum. This action is only applied to TCP and UDP packets. This can provide the better packet level control, to work with some specific use cases.

Table 2.3 Summary of modify actions.

Chapter Three
Openflow Internals

This chapter dives into the various events that trigger different kinds of packets. The triggers are discussed in detail, and the packets exchanged because of those triggers are discussed briefly here but in more length in Chapter Five. The events are discussed in the form of ladder diagrams so that the sequence of events can be easily visualized. The fact that each event is shown discretely does not mean that in real OpenFlow operations these events happen discretely; in this chapter, they are shown separately to more easily explain them.

The event examples are taken with the assumption that there is a single OpenFlow switch connected to the OpenFlow controller.

3.1   Connection Establishment Event

This event is to explain how the switch makes the connection with the OpenFlow controller and the sequence of packets, which are needed for a successful connection. It also explains the first packet exchange after the connection is established. In Figure 3.1, a simple event of connection establishment is shown. The markers on the figure label different triggers and messages (packet). The explanations of these labels are given in various steps.

Step A

When a new OpenFlow switch or a new OpenFlow controller comes up, the connection initiates with a TCP three-way handshake procedure. The TCP port number used is 6633. This step shows the three-way handshake happening.

Step B

Once the TCP connection is over, the hello packet is sent. The hello packet is a symmetric packet in OpenFlow protocol. The hello packet has no content in it; the OpenFlow generic header is the only content for hello packet, with "Type Value = 0."

Step C

Once the hellos are exchanged, the connection is established between the OpenFlow controller and OpenFlow switch. It can be checked with controller GUI or switch CLI, based upon vendor implementation. In a typical controller, the switch should be visible in the GUI.

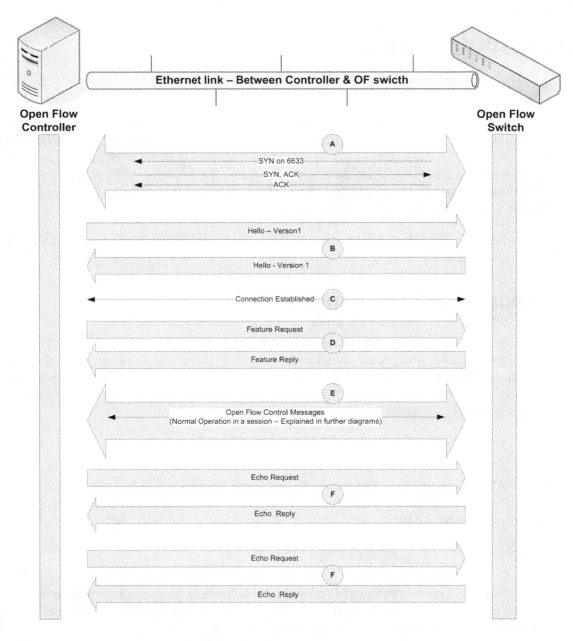

Figure 3.1 Connection establishments between OpenFlow controller and OpenFlow switch.

Step D

Feature request. This is the controller <-> switch message that is sent by the controller to determine the switch capabilities and all other feature-specific items running on OpenFlow switch. The packet has no content, and a OpenFlow generic header is used for feature request, with "Type Value = 5."

Feature reply. This is the controller <-> switch message that is sent by the switch to the controller. This packet specifies details about the OpenFlow switch. The contents carried in this packet are:

- Data path ID
- Number of flow table
- Available number of packets that can be buffered
- Switch capabilities
- Supported action flags
- Port descriptions

Step E

Once the controller knows the switch capabilities, all OpenFlow protocol–specific actions can start. The details of those actions are listed in subsequent event diagrams.

Step F

Echo request and echo reply are symmetric types of packets in OpenFlow. These are used as keep-alive messages between the OpenFlow controller and OpenFlow switch. Typically the OpenFlow header is used for echo request ("Type Value = 2") and for echo reply ("Type Value = 3"). The payload of echo request and echo reply can be changed based on implementations by different vendors.

3.2 Packet-In Event

This event explains the triggers and content of the packet-in event. In Figure 3.2, a simple isolated event of packet-in is shown. The markers on the figure label different triggers and messages (packet). The explanations of these labels are given in the text.

Step A

A connection is established per the TCP followed by hello, and feature request/reply phases. The assumption for any packet-in event to happen is that the connection has to be developed in advance.

Step B

This step explains what the trigger would be from the switch for a packet-in event. Packet-in type of event is generated when a packet is received by an OpenFlow switch and there is no match in the flow table *or* the packet matches one of the entries with the action of sending output to controller.

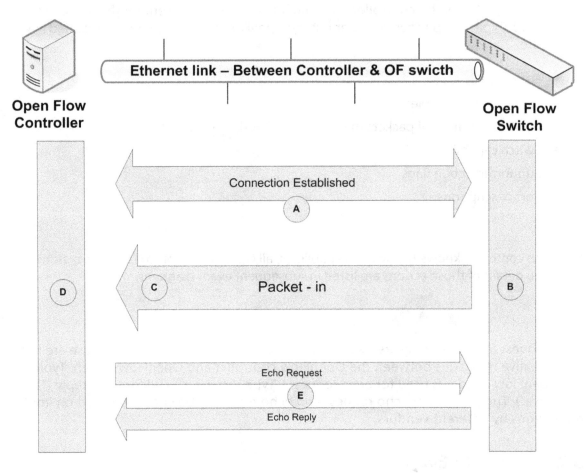

Open Flow Controller

Open Flow Switch

Connection Established

A

Packet - in

D   C   B

Echo Request

E

Echo Reply

Ethernet link – Between Controller & OF swicth

Figure 3.2 Packet-in event.

Step C

Once the packet-in condition is triggered on the switch, the packet-in event is constructed and sent to the controller.

Packet-in header contains the following:

- Buffer ID
- Packet length

- Input port
- Reason
  - 0: No match
  - 1: Flow table mentions to send packet to controller explicitly
- Data frame—the actual packet the OpenFlow switch received

Step D

The controller gets the packet-in message and strips the OpenFlow header. The packet-in field gives the information about the packet, which is coming encapsulated in that particular packet-in. After getting the packet-in information, the controller looks at the original packet and processes it as needed.

Step E

Echo request/echo reply remains parallel as keep-alive on the Ethernet link, connecting the OpenFlow controller and OpenFlow Switch.

3.3   Packet-Out Event

This section explains the triggers and content of the packet-out event. In Figure 3.3, a simple isolated event of packet-out is shown. The markers on the figure label different triggers and messages (packet). The explanations of these labels are given within this section.

Step A

Connection is established per the TCP followed by, hello, and feature request/reply phases. For any packet-out event to happen, the connection has to be developed in advance.

Step B

When the controller wants to send out any packet to a switch, it triggers a packet-out event, and the packet is sent to the switch. The trigger of this could be the reply of the controller <-> switch messages or some explicit messages sent by the controller. Typically this message is triggered if the controller wants to specify an action to a particular port of a switch.

Step C

The packet is sent from the controller to the switch. The details are in packet-out type, encapsulated in OpenFlow header. The details of OpenFlow packet-out carrier are:

- Buffer ID
- Ingress port number

- Action list (added as action descriptors)
  - Output action descriptor
  - VLAN VID action descriptor
  - VLAN PCP action descriptor
  - Strip VLAN tag action descriptor
  - Ethernet address action descriptor
  - IPv4 address action descriptor
  - IPv4 DSCP action descriptor
  - TCP/UDP port action descriptor
  - Enqueue action descriptor
  - Vendor action descriptor
- Data frame

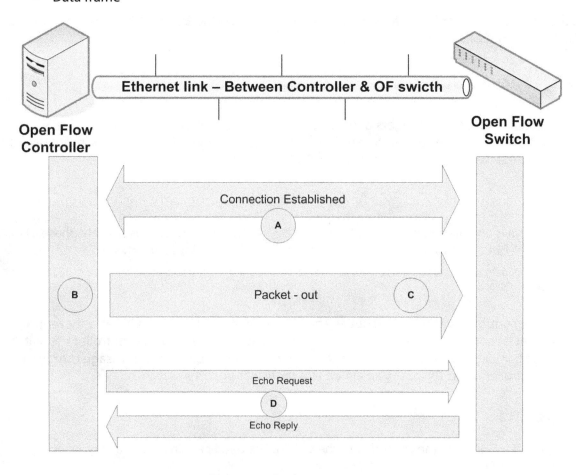

Figure 3.3 Packet–out event.

Step D

Echo request/echo reply remains parallel as keep-alive on the Ethernet link, connecting the OpenFlow controller and OpenFlow Switch.

3.4 Port Status Message Event

This section explains the triggers and content of the port status message. In Figure 3.4, a simple isolated event of port status message is shown. The markers on the figure label different triggers and messages (packet). The explanations of these labels are given within this section.

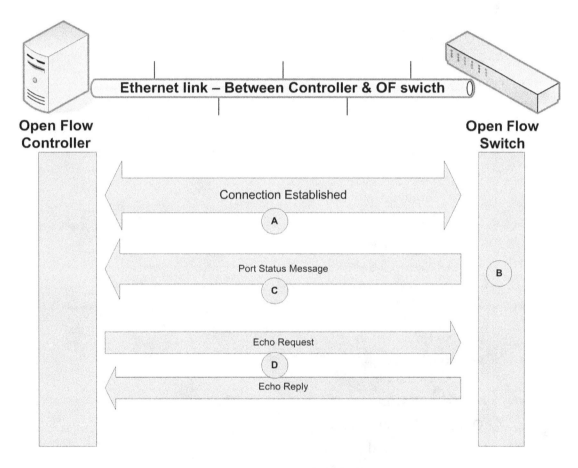

Figure 3.4 Port status message event.

Step A

Connection is established per the TCP followed by, hello, and feature request/reply phases. For any port status message/event to happen, the connection has to be developed in advance.

Step B

The trigger of sending a port status message happens when the port state is changed on the OpenFlow switch (the port goes up or down, port is added, removed, etc.), port configuration flag changes, this message is triggered by OpenFlow switch.

Step C

The switch sends the port status message, which includes:

- Reason
    - 0 Indicates add port
    - 1 Indicates add port
    - 2 Indicates modify port
- Port descriptor
    - Port number
    - Ethernet (MAC) address
    - Port description (name)
    - Port configuration flags
        - Administrator down
        - No STP
        - No receive
        - No receive STP
        - No flood
        - No forward
        - No packet-in
    - Port status flags
        - Link state
        - STP state
    - Current port feature flags
        - Link speed
        - Medium (type of link: cu, fiber, etc.)

- Auto negotiation
- Pause
  - Advertising port feature flags
    - Link speed
    - Medium (type of link: cu, fiber, etc.)
    - Auto negotiation
    - Pause
  - Supported port feature Flags
    - Link speed
    - Medium (type of link: cu, fiber, etc.)
    - Auto negotiation
    - Pause
  - Link layer neighbor advertising port feature flags
    - Link speed
    - Medium (type of link: cu, fiber, etc.)
    - Auto negotiation
    - Pause

Step D

Echo request/echo reply remains parallel as keep-alive on the Ethernet link, connecting the OpenFlow controller and the OpenFlow switch.

3.5   Set Configuration Event

This section explains the triggers and content of the set configuration message. In Figure 3.5, a simple isolated event of set configuration is shown. The markers on the figure label different triggers and messages (packet).

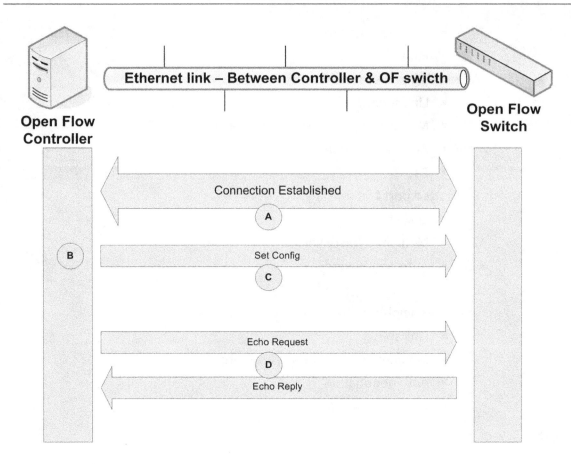

Figure 3.5 Set configuration event.

Step A

Connection is established per the TCP followed by, hello, and feature request/reply phases. For any set configuration event to happen, the connection has to be developed in advance.

Step B

Set configuration packet is triggered when the OpenFlow controller sets the configuration in the OpenFlow switch.

Step C

When the controller has to change the configurations on the switch, it will send a set-configuration message. It is a controller <-> switch message. The set-configuration message includes:

- Switch configuration flags
- Miss send length
    - Indicates maximum octets of new flow that should be sent to the controller; default value is 128

Step D

Echo request/echo reply remains parallel as keep-alive on the Ethernet link, connecting the OpenFlow controller and OpenFlow switch.

3.6   Get Configuration Request and Reply Event

This event explains the triggers and content of the configuration request/reply messages. In Figure 3.6, a simple isolated event of get configuration request/reply is shown. The markers on the figure label different triggers and messages (packet).

Step A

Connection is established per the TCP followed by, hello, and feature request/reply phases. The connection has to be developed in advance for any get configuration request/reply event to happen.

Step B

When the controller has to get the configuration in the switch, it will send the message of "Get Config."

Step C

The packet for get-configuration request contains no payload (it only contains the OpenFlow generic header); the OpenFlow switch recognizes the packet with "Type Code = 7."

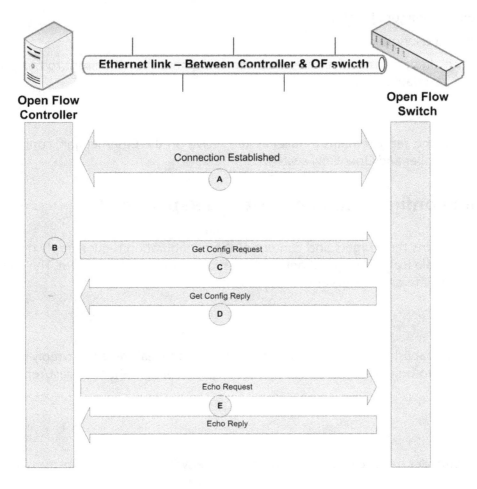

Figure 3.6 Configuration request and configuration reply event.

Step D

The switch replies with a get-configuration reply message, which contains all configurations on the switch. It is a controller <-> switch message. The get-configuration reply message includes:

- Switch configuration flags
- Miss send length
- Indicates maximum octets of new flow that should be sent to the controller; default value is 128

Step E

Echo request/echo reply remains parallel as keep-alive on the Ethernet link, connecting the OpenFlow controller and OpenFlow switch.

3.7   Flow-Modification Event

This section explains the triggers and content of the flow-modification messages. In Figure 3.7, a simple isolated event of flow modification is shown. The markers on the figure label different triggers and messages (packet).

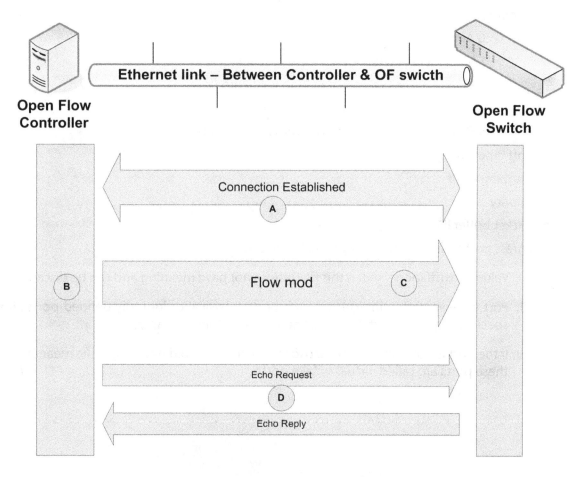

Figure 3.7 Flow modification event.

Step A

Connection is established per the TCP followed by, hello, and feature request/reply phases. The connection has to be developed in advance for any flow-modification event to happen.

Step B

The controller triggers this packet, with a detailed set of actions in it, when the controller has to add/modify/delete a flow table in the switch.

Step C

The flow-modification packet contains the following information:

- Flow match descriptor
  - Mainly twelve tuples
- Command
  - 0 Add new flow
  - 1 Modify all matching flows
  - 2 Modify entries strictly matching wild-card flows
  - 3 Delete all matching flows
  - 4 Delete strictly matched wild cards and priority
- Soft time-out
- Hard time-out
- Priority
- Packet buffer ID
- Egress port Number (this is only used for delete)

  I. Value of oxffff (none) mean this fields does not have meaning and can be discarded

  II. Port oxoooo–oxffoo indicates switch ports (physical or logically defined ports); it specifies a specific port if the port number is within this range

  III. If the port is not from the range oxoooo–oxffoo, it could have a specific meaning—these ports are called virtual or fake ports

Table 3.1 explains different types of port numbers.

Range	Description	Port Set
0x0000	Reserved	Reserved
0x0001 - 0xff00	Switch ports	Actual port number
0xfff8	Send the packet back on the port where it is received.	In-Port
0xfff9	Perform actions in flow table, only for PACKET_OUT message.	Table
0xfffa	Process the packet using the traditional L2/L3 switching.	Normal
0xfffb	Flood the packet except incoming port.	Flood
0xfffc	Send the packet out all ports except ingress and on STP disabled ports.	All
0xfffd	Send the packet to the controller.	Controller
0xfffe	Send the packet to all switch local OpenFlow ports.	Local
0xffff	Not a physical port in switch.	None

Table 3.1

- Flags
    - Send flow removed
    - Check overlap
    - Emergency flow
- Action list (added as action descriptors)
    - Output action descriptor
    - VLAN VID action descriptor
    - VLAN PCP action descriptor
    - Strip VLAN tag action descriptor

- o Ethernet address action descriptor
- o IPv4 address action descriptor
- o IPv4 DSCP action descriptor
- o TCP/UDP Port action descriptor
- o Enqueue action descriptor
- o Vendor action descriptor

Step D

Echo request/echo reply remains parallel as keep-alive on the Ethernet link, connecting the OpenFlow controller and OpenFlow switch.

3.8 Flow-Removed Event

This section explains the triggers and content of the flow-remove messages. In Figure 3.8, a simple isolated event of flow remove is shown. The markers on the figure label different triggers and messages (packet).

Step A

Connection is established per the TCP followed by, hello, and feature request/reply phase. The connection has to be developed in advance for any flow-remove event to happen.

Step B

The controller triggers this packet when it has to delete a flow table in the switch. This step is necessary only if the flow-remove event is triggered by the controller.

Step C

If the flow delete is triggered by the controller (if step B is true), only this packet is sent. The packet is similar to any flow-modify packet (as explained in the flow-modify event section), but it will have a command set to 3 or 4, which signals that this flow modify is to remove the flow.

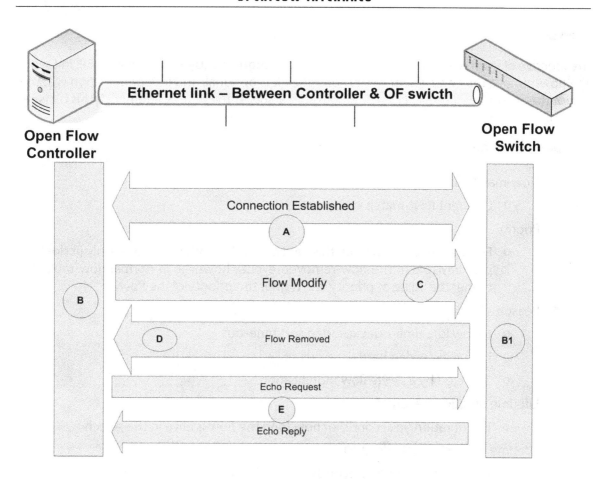

Figure 3.8 Flow-removed event.

Step B1

This step is necessary if the flow is being deleted because of a hard or idle time-out" is expired on a particular flow, and the send-flow-remove flag is set for the flow entry at the time of addition.

Step D

Irrespective of from where the flow delete request is triggered (by Step B or Step-B1), in Step D, the flow-remove message is sent to the controller. It is optional, and it depends upon whether or not the send-flow-remove flag is or is not set in a flow at the time of addition. If this bit is set, then the flow remove message is sent—otherwise this packet will not be sent.

This packet includes:

- Flow-match descriptors
  - Different flow-match variables
- Priority
  - For flow-removed packet, this field is for information purposes only (it does not play any role in the flow-removed event), however, in normal flow table, the higher the value of priority, the higher the priority of the flow
- Reason
  - 0 Flow idle time-out exceeded soft time-out.
  - 1 Time exceeded hard time-out.
  - 2 Evicted by a *delete* flow modification.
- Lifetime duration (seconds)
  - The duration (in seconds) of how long the flow is alive in the switch
- Lifetime duration (nanoseconds)
  - The duration (in nanoseconds) of how long the flow is alive in the switch
- Soft time-out
  - The soft time-out from original flow modification
- Number of packets transferred
  - Number of packets that have hit the flow entry
- Number of bytes transferred
  - Number of bytes that have hit the flow entry

Step E

Echo request/echo reply remains parallel as keep-alive on the Ethernet link, connecting the OpenFlow controller and OpenFlow switch.

3.9   Port-Modify Event

This section explains the triggers and content of the port-modify messages. In Figure 3.9, a simple isolated event of port modify is shown. The markers on the figure label different triggers and messages (packet).

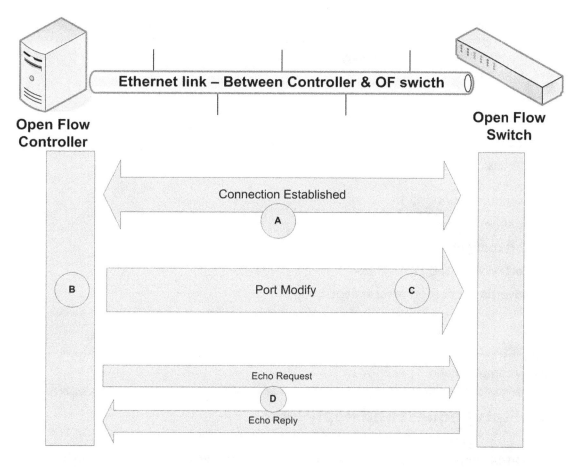

Figure 3.9 Port modify event.

Step A

Connection is established per the TCP followed by, hello, and feature request/reply phases. This is the assumption, as, for any Port Modify event to happen, the connection has to be developed in advance.

Step B

The trigger happens when the controller (administrator) changes port configuration flags—such as "admin down," "no STP," "no receive," "no receive STP," "no flood," "no FWD," or "no packet-in"—from the controller.

Step C

The port modification message has the following fields in the packet, and, using these fields, the port properties can be modified:

- Port number
- Ethernet address
- Port configuration flags
- Port configuration flags mask
- Advertisement (port feature flags)

Step D

Echo request/echo reply remains parallel as keep-alive on the Ethernet link, connecting the OpenFlow controller and OpenFlow switch.

3.10   Stats Request and Reply Event

This section explains the triggers and content of the stats request/reply messages. In Figure 3.10, a simple isolated event of stats request/reply is shown. The markers on the figure label different triggers and messages (packet).

Step A

Connection is established per the TCP followed by, hello, and feature request/reply phases. This is the assumption, as, for any stats request/reply event to happen, the connection has to be developed in advance.

Step B

When the controller wants to poll the switch for knowing different kinds of statistics, this message is triggered.

Step D

The statistics packet includes:

- Type
    - 0 OpenFlow switch description
    - 1 Information of individual flow
    - 2 Information of aggregated flow
    - 3 Statistical information of flow table
    - 4 Information of port statistics
    - 5 Information on queue statistics
    - 65535 vendor extensions
- Flags
    - Should be zero in value
- Stats Body
    - Different body for different type value

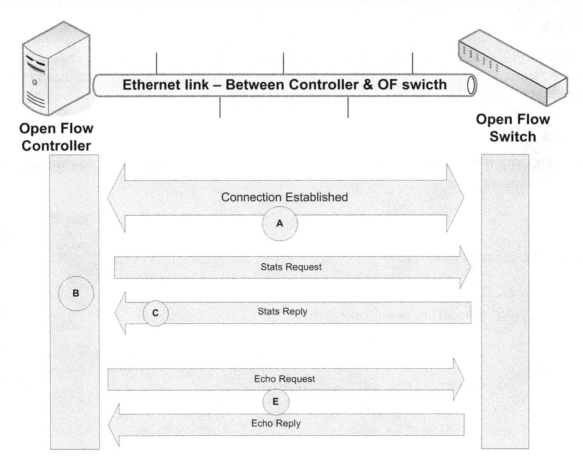

Figure 3.10 Statistics request and reply event.

Step E

Echo request/echo reply remains parallel as keep-alive on the Ethernet link, connecting the OpenFlow controller and OpenFlow switch.

3.11   Barrier Request and Reply Event

This section explains the triggers and content of the barrier request/reply messages. In Figure 3.11, a simple isolated event of barrier request/reply is shown. The markers on the figure label different triggers and messages (packet).

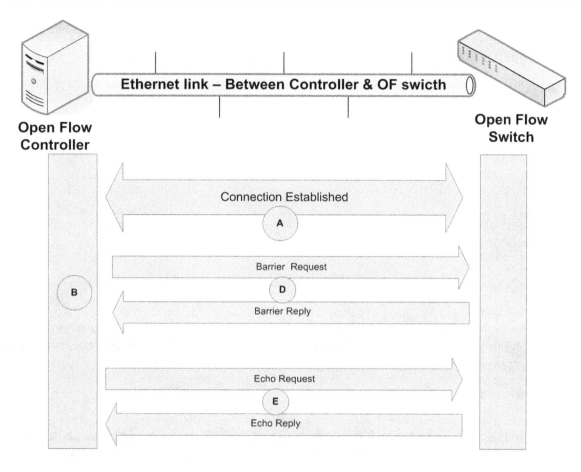

Figure 3.11 Barrier request and reply.

Step A

Connection is established per the TCP followed by, hello, and feature request/reply phases. This is the assumption, as, for any barrier request/reply event to happen, the connection has to be developed in advance.

Step B

When the controller wants to make sure that all given tasks to the OpenFlow switch have been completed or to know when the tasks will be done, it triggers this barrier-request message.

Step D

Barrier request message is just an OpenFlow header message with "Type Value = 19."

The switch looks at the barrier message and triggers a barrier-reply message when the tasks assigned by the controller are done.

Barrier-reply message is just an OpenFlow header message with "Type Value = 20," with the XID of barrier-request message.

Step E

Echo request/echo reply remains parallel as keep-alive on the Ethernet link, connecting the OpenFlow controller and OpenFlow switch.

3.12   Queue Get Configuration Request and Reply Event

This section explains the triggers and content of the queue get configuration request/reply messages. In Figure 3.12, a simple isolated event of queue get configuration request/reply is shown. The markers on the figure label different triggers and messages (packet).

Step A

Connection is established per the TCP followed by, hello, and feature request/reply phases. This is the assumption, as, for any get queue configuration request/reply event to happen, the connection has to be developed in advance.

Step B

When the controller wants to poll the queuing configuration on the port of the OpenFlow switch, this message is triggered.

Step C

The queuing request contains the port number on which the queuing information is requested. The queuing configuration-reply message contains the port number and the queuing information configured on that port.

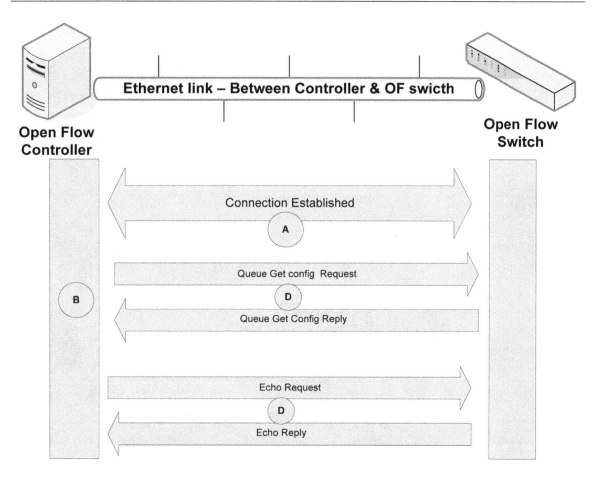

Figure 3.12 Queue get configuration request and reply.

Step D

Echo request/echo reply remains parallel as keep-alive on the Ethernet link, connecting the OpenFlow controller and OpenFlow switch.

3.13   Error Event

This section explains the triggers and content of error messages. In Figure 3.13, a simple isolated event of error message is shown. The markers on the figure label different triggers and messages (packet).

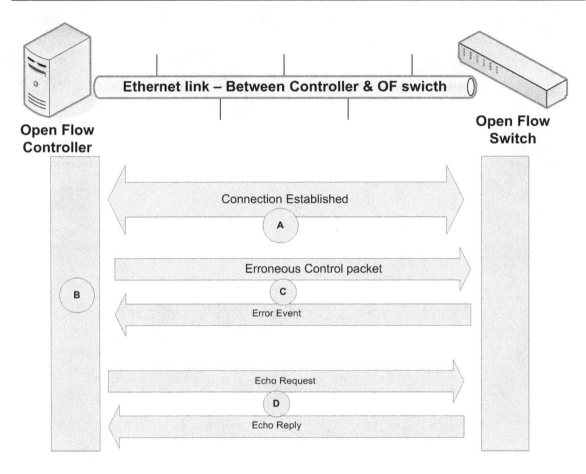

Figure 3.13 Error event.

Step A

Connection is established per the TCP followed by, hello, and feature request/reply phases. The connection has to be developed in advance for any error event to happen. However, the error can happen in the hello packet itself.

Step B

The error event is typically generated when a controller sends a packet that is not understandable or supported or the switch fails to process it. So the trigger could be any control packet sent to the switch.

Step C

If the OpenFlow switch does not understand or support or failed to process the OpenFlow control packet sent by the controller, it sends the error packet to the controller, specifying the cause of the error. The packet contains type and code values that specify the error in detail.

Step D

Echo request/echo reply remains parallel as keep-alive on the Ethernet link, connecting the OpenFlow controller and OpenFlow switch.

Chapter Four
OpenFlow Case Study

This chapter focuses on a simple OpenFlow setup to study the basic protocol in action. The setup (which has three switches in it) has triangle connections between its three switches, and each switch is reachable by the OpenFlow controller on the management network. The links between the three switches are made of different cost, so we can easily analyze how OpenFlow calculates the shortest path and how the reinstallation of flow happens in case of failures. To explain it better, some wire-shark captures are also taken and labeled with relevant information. The flow of the case study starts with the very first step of discovering the OpenFlow-based switch network.

4.1 Discovery of Topology

The very first step of an OpenFlow-based network is the discovery of OpenFlow switches by OpenFlow controller. The controller needs to know the topology before it can actually look for the path between two different hosts in an OpenFlow network and install any flow for data-plane traffic.

The OpenFlow controller learns about the OpenFlow-based switches by listening on TCP port number 6633. Once the OpenFlow controller knows about the OpenFlow switch, the next step is to discover the total view of the network (i.e., knowing the individual OpenFlow switch details and the actual links and ports connected between different OpenFlow switches). This discovery is done in two steps: step one is to know about the individual switches, and step two is to know about the links between those switches.

Step one is taken care of by the feature request and feature reply mechanism. The controller sends a feature-request message as soon as the TCP handshake is done. The newly connected switch replies with a feature-reply message. The feature-reply message tells the controller about the switch capabilities, ports details, and action capabilities. In the second step, the inter switch links (connections between OpenFlow switches) discovery happens using LLDP frames that are sent on all connected (up) ports of the switches (or all ports, depending on implementation) between different OpenFlow switches.

How are the LLDP frames sent? By definition of OpenFlow protocol, the switch does not understand LLDP, so all the LLDP frames are actually made by the controller and sent by using a packet-out event from the controller, with an action to send on all or up state ports. The incoming LLDP packets on connected ports on peer switch are encapsulated in packet-in headers and sent to the controller by switches. Once the controller has all packets with it, it will have a view of the full topology (after it processes various LLDP packets coming from various OpenFlow switches). (Note that the iteration of LLDP is every ten seconds.)

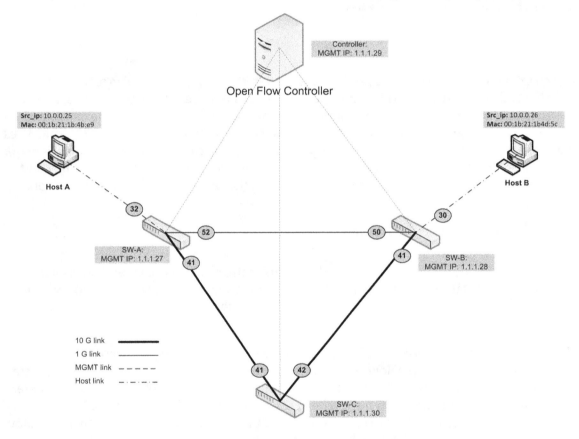

Figure 4.1

Based on the above steps, the controller can have the view of topology shown in Figure 4.1. (Note that the controller still would not know the external hosts, as shown in Figure 4.1.)

Whole operation of topology discovery can be listed in the following steps (for the topology discovery explained in Figure 4.1):

Packet initiated from:	Packet destined to:	Packet type	Packet payload and details
Controller	All switches	Feature request	Controller send feature request to all switches
All switches	Controller	Feature reply	All switches send the feature-reply message (explaining all features supported by the switch)
Controller	SW-A	Packet-out	Controller asks SW-A to send LLDP packets on port 32, 52, 41 of SW-A
Controller	SW-B	Packet-out	Controller asks SW- B to send LLDP packets on port 30, 50, 41 of SW-B
Controller	SW-C	Packet-out	Controller asks SW-C to send LLDP packets on port 42, 41 of SW-C
SW-A	Controller	Packet-in	SW-A sends the encapsulated LLDP packet, which it received from SW-B on port -52
SW-A	Controller	Packet-in	SW-A sends the encapsulated LLDP packet, which it received from SW-C on port -41
SW-B	Controller	Packet-in	SW-B sends the encapsulated LLDP packet, which it received from SW-A on port -50
SW-B	Controller	Packet-in	SW-B sends the encapsulated LLDP packet, which it received from SW-C on port -41
SW-C	Controller	Packet-in	SW-C sends the encapsulated LLDP packet, which it received from SW-A on port -41
SW-C	Controller	Packet-in	SW-C sends the encapsulated LLDP packet, which it received from SW-B on port -42

Table 4.1

4.2   Calculation of Shortest Path

Once the controller knows the topology, the shortest path can be calculated. This book explains the shortest-path calculation based on Diskstra (the same as traditional STP). Once the shortest paths are collected between end nodes, the port modification commands are used to program the ports in OpenFlow switches. By the port modification commands, the ports are programmed with the action to forward a packet or drop. By doing this, even if the switch receives a packet with an action of flooding, it will flood to only the ports that are part of shortest path.

As of now, the calculations are based on the bandwidths of the links. Here is one example of how it can be implemented in the topology shown in Figure 4.1:

As per the example we have taken, let us say that the packet needs to be sent between host A and host B, and there are two paths that can be taken. Let us say here is the cost for links in each path:

1.   SW-A <-> SW-B = 1G

2.   SW-A <-> SW-C <-> SW-B = all 10G

Based on the shortest path algorithm, here is how the event will happen:

1.   When the network comes up, the controller will send the message "port modification" by putting a port flag of no flooding on ports SW-A, SW-B, and SW-C.

   a.   SW-A will get "port_mod" for port (32, 52, 41)—putting a "no flooding" flag on all ports

   b.   SW-B will get "port_mod" for port (30, 50, 41)—putting a "no flooding" flag on all ports

   c.   SW-C will get "port_mod" for port (41, 42)—putting a "no flooding" flag on all ports

2.   Once the controller determines the topology using LLDP packet in/out, the shortest path tree will be calculated, and few links per switch will be enabled again by using the port modification packet.

   a.   SW-A will get "port_mod" for port (32, 41), putting the port in forwarding state

   b.   SW-B will get "port_mod" for port (41, 30), putting the port in forwarding state

   c.   SW-C will get "port_mod" for port (41, 42), putting the port in forwarding state

Figure 4.2 shows the shortest path calculated by the controller after both steps are completed.

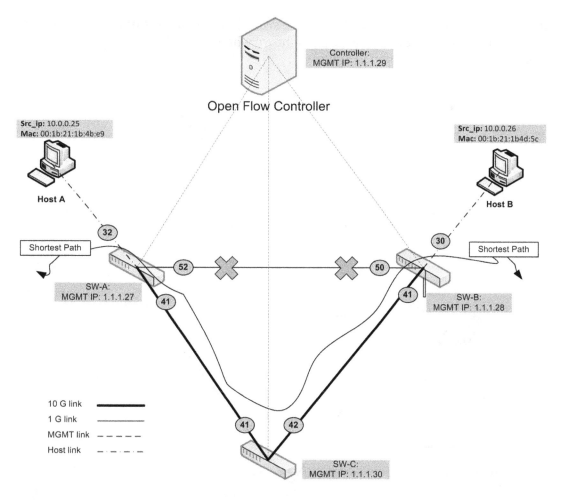

Figure 4.2

If the link speed between SW-A and SW-B is changed to one hundred gigabytes, then the port status flags will change the topology view at the controller, and the recalculation of the shortest path will happen, which will trigger the "port_mod" packet again, based on the changed topology.

4.3 Flow Table Buildup with Example of Ping Traffic

To demonstrate a simple flow installation on the switch, a ping example has been taken, wherein host A would ping to host B. In Figure 4.3, it is shown where all the flow would add up, given this is the shortest path, as explained in Figure 4.2.

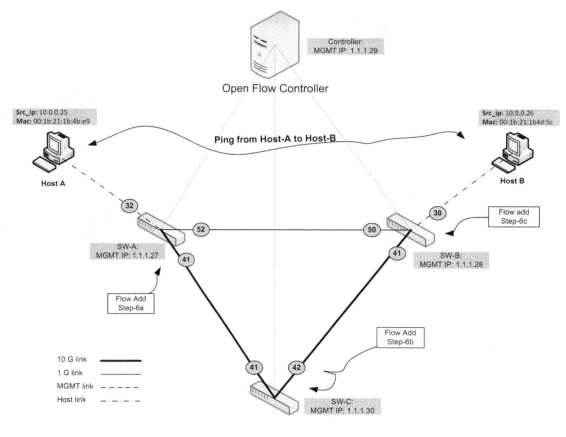

Figure 4.3

The operation of flow installation will happen in the following steps.

Step 1

When a ping command is executed from host A to ping host B on 10.0.0.26, an ARP request will be generated by host A, which it will send to SW-A. When SW-A gets the ARP request, it will send a packet (which will have the ARP request encapsulated in it) to the controller.

The packet in Figure 4.4 shows how it will look on the wire.

```
▷ Internet Protocol, Src:  1.1.1.27 , Dst:  1.1.1.29
▷ Transmission Control Protocol, Src Port: 53706 (53706), Dst Port: 6633 (6633), Seq: 9, Ack: 531, Len: 78
▽ OpenFlow Protocol  ═══════════════▶   ARP request encapsulated in OF Packet In
  ▷ Header
  ▽ Packet In
      Buffer ID: 4294967295
      Frame Total Length: 60
      Frame Recv Port: 32  ═══════════▶  The incoming port for this ARP request
      Reason Sent: Action explicitly output to controller (1)
  ▽ Frame Data: FFFFFFFFFFFF001B211B4BE9080600010800060400010001B...
    ▷ Ethernet II, Src: IntelCor_1b:4b:e9 (00:1b:21:1b:4b:e9), Dst: Broadcast (ff:ff:ff:ff:ff:ff)
    ▽ Address Resolution Protocol (request) ═══════════▶   Actual ARP Request
        Hardware type: Ethernet (0x0001)
        Protocol type: IP (0x0800)
        Hardware size: 6
        Protocol size: 4
        Opcode: request (0x0001)
        [Is gratuitous: False]
        Sender MAC address: IntelCor_1b:4b:e9 (00:1b:21:1b:4b:e9)
        Sender IP address: 10.0.0.25 (10.0.0.25)
        Target MAC address: 00:00:00_00:00:00 (00:00:00:00:00:00)
        Target IP address: 10.0.0.26 (10.0.0.26)
```

Figure 4.4

Step 2

On getting the packet-in, the controller will decapsulate the packet and see the ARP request. Controller will send a packet-out (encapsulating the original ARP request) to all edge switches with an action to send the ARP request to all edge ports. In the topology, the only edge switch is SW-B (SW-C is a pure transit switch).

How does the controller know about the non-edge switch? When LLDP exchanges happen, the LLDP packets are sent on all ports of the switch which are in up state. If the switch does not get reply of LLDP sent on "some" of up state ports, it is known that those "some" up state ports are edge ports which are connected to other than switch.

Figure 4.5 shows how this packet-out will look on the wire.

```
▷ Internet Protocol, Src: 1.1.1.29 , Dst: 1.1.1.28
▷ Transmission Control Protocol, Src Port: 6633 (6633), Dst Port: 41101 (41101), Seq: 1, Ack: 351, Len: 84
▽ OpenFlow Protocol
  ▷ Header
  ▽ Packet Out                 ══════════▶      ARP request encapsulated in OF Packet Out
      Buffer ID: None
      Frame Recv Port: None  (not associated with a physical port)
      Size of action array in bytes: 8
    ▽ Output Action(s)
      ▽ Action
          Type: Output to switch port (0)
          Len: 8
          Output port: 30   ══════════▶      Action specifies the ARP to be  sent on port 30 (Edge port)
          Max Bytes to Send: 65535
      # of Actions: 1
  ▽ Frame Data: FFFFFFFFFFFF001B211B4BE90806000108000604000010018...
    ▷ Ethernet II, Src: IntelCor_1b:4b:e9 (00:1b:21:1b:4b:e9), Dst: Broadcast (ff:ff:ff:ff:ff:ff)
    ▷ Address Resolution Protocol (request) ══════════▶    Actual Arp Request
```

Figure 4.5

Step 3

Once switch B gets the packet-out and it follows the action of forwarding the original ARP request to all edge ports, it gets a reply from host B. Switch B forwards the ARP reply to the controller, essentially sending the ARP reply in the form of packet-in to the controller, with the MAC address of 10.0.0.26. Figure 4.6 shows how it will be seen on wire.

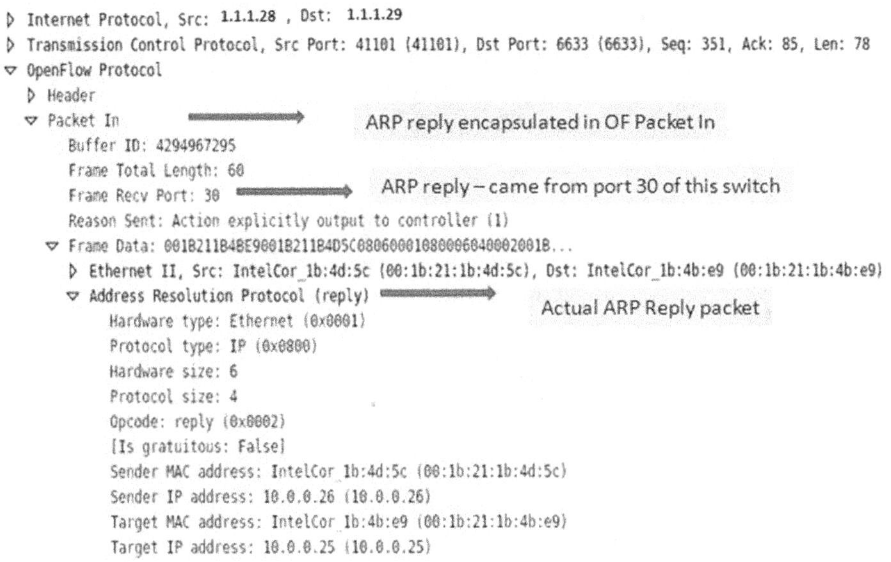

▷ Internet Protocol, Src: 1.1.1.28 , Dst: 1.1.1.29
▷ Transmission Control Protocol, Src Port: 41101 (41101), Dst Port: 6633 (6633), Seq: 351, Ack: 85, Len: 78
▽ OpenFlow Protocol
  ▷ Header
  ▽ Packet In   ➡️   ARP reply encapsulated in OF Packet In
      Buffer ID: 4294967295
      Frame Total Length: 60
      Frame Recv Port: 30   ➡️   ARP reply – came from port 30 of this switch
      Reason Sent: Action explicitly output to controller (1)
    ▽ Frame Data: 001B211B4BE9001B211B4D5C08060001080006040002001B...
      ▷ Ethernet II, Src: IntelCor_1b:4d:5c (00:1b:21:1b:4d:5c), Dst: IntelCor_1b:4b:e9 (00:1b:21:1b:4b:e9)
      ▽ Address Resolution Protocol (reply)   ➡️   Actual ARP Reply packet
          Hardware type: Ethernet (0x0001)
          Protocol type: IP (0x0800)
          Hardware size: 6
          Protocol size: 4
          Opcode: reply (0x0002)
          [Is gratuitous: False]
          Sender MAC address: IntelCor_1b:4d:5c (00:1b:21:1b:4d:5c)
          Sender IP address: 10.0.0.26 (10.0.0.26)
          Target MAC address: IntelCor_1b:4b:e9 (00:1b:21:1b:4b:e9)
          Target IP address: 10.0.0.25 (10.0.0.25)

Figure 4.6

Step 4

The controller tells switch A about the MAC address of 10.0.0.26 so that host A can populate its ARP table. The controller sends the packet-out to switch A with ARP reply embedded in it with an action to send it to host A. Figure 4.7 illustrates how it will be seen on wire.

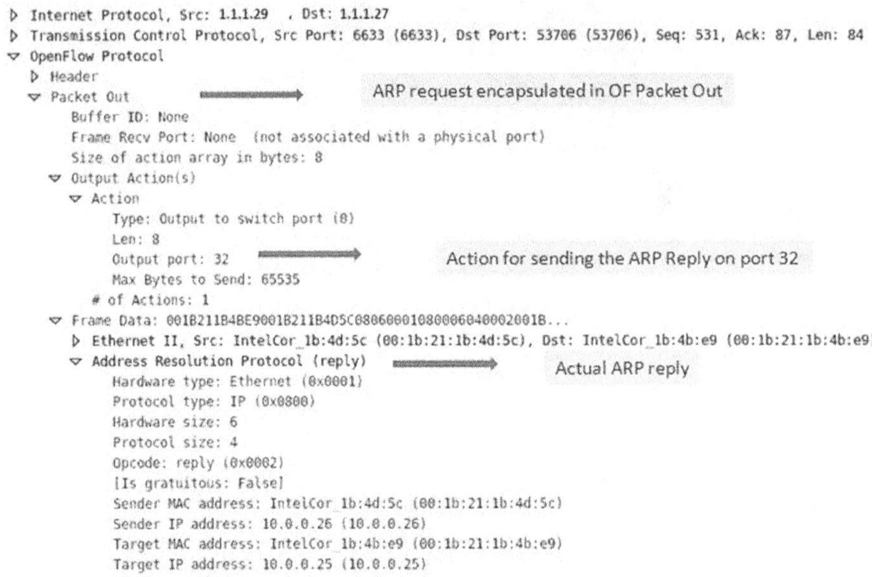

▷ Internet Protocol, Src: 1.1.1.29 , Dst: 1.1.1.27
▷ Transmission Control Protocol, Src Port: 6633 (6633), Dst Port: 53706 (53706), Seq: 531, Ack: 87, Len: 84
▽ OpenFlow Protocol
    ▷ Header
    ▽ Packet Out   ━━━━━━━▶   ARP request encapsulated in OF Packet Out
        Buffer ID: None
        Frame Recv Port: None (not associated with a physical port)
        Size of action array in bytes: 8
      ▽ Output Action(s)
        ▽ Action
            Type: Output to switch port (0)
            Len: 8
            Output port: 32   ━━━━━━▶   Action for sending the ARP Reply on port 32
            Max Bytes to Send: 65535
        # of Actions: 1
    ▽ Frame Data: 001B211B4BE9001B211B4D5C080600010800060400002001B...
        ▷ Ethernet II, Src: IntelCor_1b:4d:5c (00:1b:21:1b:4d:5c), Dst: IntelCor_1b:4b:e9 (00:1b:21:1b:4b:e9)
        ▽ Address Resolution Protocol (reply) ━━━━━━▶   Actual ARP reply
            Hardware type: Ethernet (0x0001)
            Protocol type: IP (0x0800)
            Hardware size: 6
            Protocol size: 4
            Opcode: reply (0x0002)
            [Is gratuitous: False]
            Sender MAC address: IntelCor_1b:4d:5c (00:1b:21:1b:4d:5c)
            Sender IP address: 10.0.0.26 (10.0.0.26)
            Target MAC address: IntelCor_1b:4b:e9 (00:1b:21:1b:4b:e9)
            Target IP address: 10.0.0.25 (10.0.0.25)

Figure 4.7

Step 5

Now as host A has the ARP address of 10.0.0.26, it will send the ICMP request packet to 10.0.0.26.
When this ICMP packet comes to SW-A, it will encapsulate it in a packet-in and send it to the
controller. Figure 4.8 shows how it will be on wire.

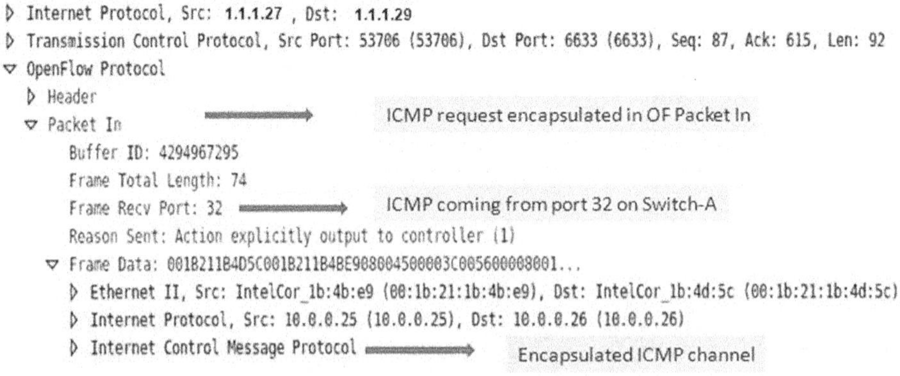

▷ Internet Protocol, Src: 1.1.1.27 , Dst: 1.1.1.29
▷ Transmission Control Protocol, Src Port: 53706 (53706), Dst Port: 6633 (6633), Seq: 87, Ack: 615, Len: 92
▽ OpenFlow Protocol
    ▷ Header
    ▽ Packet In   ━━━━━━━▶   ICMP request encapsulated in OF Packet In
        Buffer ID: 4294967295
        Frame Total Length: 74
        Frame Recv Port: 32   ━━━━━━▶   ICMP coming from port 32 on Switch-A
        Reason Sent: Action explicitly output to controller (1)
    ▽ Frame Data: 001B211B4D5C001B211B4BE908004500003C005600008001...
        ▷ Ethernet II, Src: IntelCor_1b:4b:e9 (00:1b:21:1b:4b:e9), Dst: IntelCor_1b:4d:5c (00:1b:21:1b:4d:5c)
        ▷ Internet Protocol, Src: 10.0.0.25 (10.0.0.25), Dst: 10.0.0.26 (10.0.0.26)
        ▷ Internet Control Message Protocol ━━━━━━━▶   Encapsulated ICMP channel

Figure 4.8

Step 6 (6a, 6b, and 6c)

While the ICMP request packet comes out from host-A at Step 5, at the same time, the controller starts installing the flow (by now it knows the MAC address from ARP learning). Flow-modification packets are sent by the controller to switches A, B, and C to install the flow bidirectionally on each switch. Here is the example of flow modification on switch A (similar packets will go out from the controller for installing entries in switches B and C).

```
▷ Internet Protocol, Src: 1.1.1.29 , Dst:  1.1.1.27
▷ Transmission Control Protocol, Src Port: 6633 (6633), Dst Port: 53706 (53706), Seq: 615, Ack: 179, Len: 80
▽ OpenFlow Protocol
  ▷ Header
  ▽ Flow Modification          ════════════▶  Flow Mod packet for matching any packet coming on port 41,
    ▽ Match                                    With MAC address of Host-A and Host-B.
      ▷ Match Types
        Input Port: 41
        Ethernet Src Addr: IntelCor_1b:4d:5c (00:1b:21:1b:4d:5c)
        Ethernet Dst Addr: IntelCor_1b:4b:e9 (00:1b:21:1b:4b:e9)
        Input VLAN ID: 65535
        IP Src Addr: 0.0.0.0 (0.0.0.0)
        IP Dst Addr: 0.0.0.0 (0.0.0.0)
      Cookie: 0xc00261a80002c4b8
      Command: Modify entry strictly matching wildcards (2)
      Idle Time (sec) Before Discarding: 300
      Max Time (sec) Before Discarding: 0
      Priority: 25000
      Buffer ID: None
      Out Port (delete* only): 0
    ▷ Flags
    ▽ Output Action(s)
    ▽ Action
        Type: Output to switch port (0)
        Len: 8
        Output port: 32      ════════════▶  Output to the switch port – 32, when the match happens.
        Max Bytes to Send: 0
      # of Actions: 1
```

Figure 4.9

Step 7

The packet-in that was sent to the controller by switch A, encapsulating the ICMP request, will be sent to switch B (by the controller) encapsulated in packet-out.

Step 8

The reply of the ICMP packet will be sent by switch B to switch A based on the flow installed in Steps 6a, 6b, and 6c. (Note that, as explained in Section 4.2, the shortest path between switch A and switch B will be via switch C.)

4.4   Flow Table Modification with Failover Example

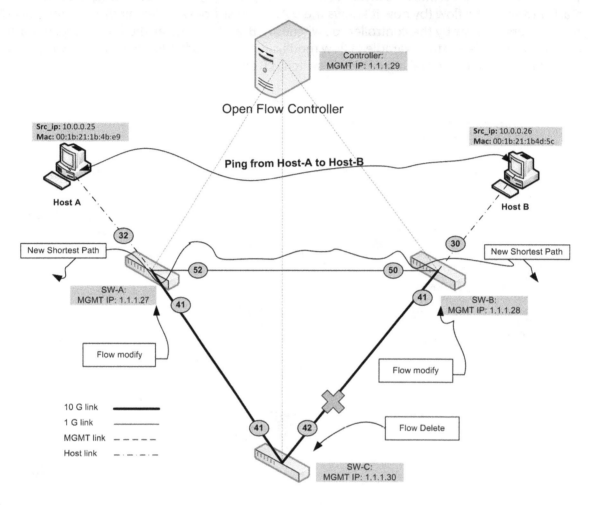

Figure 4.10

As shown in Figure 4.2, the shortest path is based on the better bandwidth (SW-A <-> SW-B <-> SW-C). For doing failover, the link between switch C and switch B can be broken (Figure 4.10), forcing the flow modification to happen. The new flow will be modified and installed in the switch network, as explained in below steps.

Step 1

When the link between Switch C and switch B is broken (by shutting it down on switch C), switch C sends a port-status message to the controller. Figure 4.11 shows how this message will appear on wire.

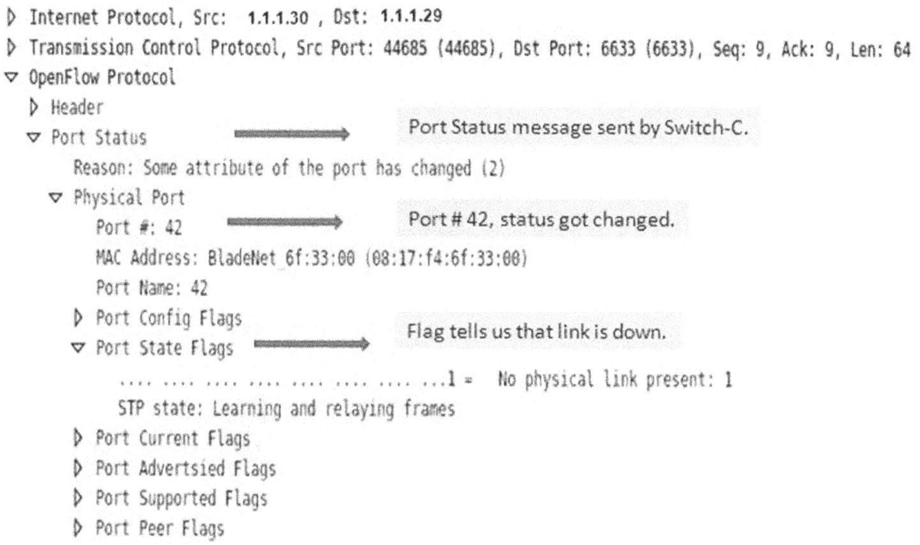

```
▷ Internet Protocol, Src:  1.1.1.30 , Dst: 1.1.1.29
▷ Transmission Control Protocol, Src Port: 44685 (44685), Dst Port: 6633 (6633), Seq: 9, Ack: 9, Len: 64
▽ OpenFlow Protocol
  ▷ Header
  ▽ Port Status          ━━━━━▶       Port Status message sent by Switch-C.
      Reason: Some attribute of the port has changed (2)
    ▽ Physical Port
        Port #: 42        ━━━━━▶       Port # 42, status got changed.
        MAC Address: BladeNet 6f:33:00 (08:17:f4:6f:33:00)
        Port Name: 42
      ▷ Port Config Flags
      ▽ Port State Flags  ━━━━━▶       Flag tells us that link is down.
          .... .... .... .... .... .... .... ...1 =   No physical link present: 1
          STP state: Learning and relaying frames
      ▷ Port Current Flags
      ▷ Port Advertsied Flags
      ▷ Port Supported Flags
      ▷ Port Peer Flags
```

Figure 4.11

Step 2

When the controller gets the information on the broken link, it does the shortest path calculation again, and it sends the flow-modification messages for installing a new path. (As per the topology, the new path would be the direct one-gigabyte link between switch A and switch B.) Figure 4.12 shows the capture of the flow-modification message for switch B on the wire.

◁ Internet Protocol, Src: **1.1.1.29** , Dst: **1.1.1.28**
◁ Transmission Control Protocol, Src Port: 6633 (6633), Dst Port: 41101 (41101), Seq: 190, Ack: 9, Len: 80
▽ OpenFlow Protocol
  ◁ Header
  ▽ Flow Modification
    ▽ Match
     ◁ Match Types
      Input Port: 30   ━━━━━━▶   Match any packet coming on port 30
      Ethernet Src Addr: IntelCor_1b:4d:5c (00:1b:21:1b:4d:5c)
      Ethernet Dst Addr: IntelCor_1b:4b:e9 (00:1b:21:1b:4b:e9)
      Input VLAN ID: 65535
      IP Src Addr: 0.0.0.0 (0.0.0.0)
      IP Dst Addr: 0.0.0.0 (0.0.0.0)
    Cookie: 0xc00261a80002c4b8
    Command: Modify entry strictly matching wildcards (2)
    Idle Time (sec) Before Discarding: 300
    Max Time (sec) Before Discarding: 0
    Priority: 25000
    Buffer ID: None
    Out Port (delete* only): 0
  ◁ Flags
  ▽ Output Action(s)
    ▽ Action
      Type: Output to switch port (0)
      Len: 8
      Output port: 50   ━━━━━━▶   When the match happens, send that packet to port #50.
      Max Bytes to Send: 0   <This is a flow change, earlier it was port #41>
    # of Actions: 1

Figure 4.12

Step 3

As the controller knows now that there is no link between switches C and B, the flow that was configured on switch C's flow table will be deleted. Here is the flow-modification packet that will be sent for modifying the flow. Figure 4.13 shows the packet on the wire. (Similarly, the flow will be modified on switches A and B.)

```
▷ Internet Protocol, Src:  1.1.1.29 , Dst:  1.1.1.30
▷ Transmission Control Protocol, Src Port: 6633 (6633), Dst Port: 44685 (44685), Seq: 9, Ack: 73, Len: 72
▽ OpenFlow Protocol
  ▷ Header
  ▽ Flow Modification
    ▽ Match
      ▷ Match Types                                          Match entry with input port 40
        Input Port: 42           ═══════════════▶           (port which is now down)
        Ethernet Src Addr: IntelCor 1b:4d:5c (00:1b:21:1b:4d:5c)
        Ethernet Dst Addr: IntelCor 1b:4b:e9 (00:1b:21:1b:4b:e9)
        Input VLAN ID: 65535
        IP Src Addr: 0.0.0.0 (0.0.0.0)
        IP Dst Addr: 0.0.0.0 (0.0.0.0)
      Cookie: 0xc00261a80002c4b8
      Command: Delete entry strictly matching wildcards and priority (4)  ═══════▶  Command to delete the flow
      Idle Time (sec) Before Discarding: 300
      Max Time (sec) Before Discarding: 0
      Priority: 25000
      Buffer ID: None
      Out Port (delete* only): None  (not associated with a physical port)
    ▽ Flags
        .... .... .... ...1 = Send flow removed: Yes (1)
        .... .... .... ..0. = Check for overlap before adding flow: No (0)
        .... .... .... .0.. = Install flow into emergecy flow table: No (0)
    ▽ Output Action(s)
        Warning: No actions were specified
```

Figure 4.13

The steps explained in Section 4.1 through 4.4 can be applied to any bigger deployment to understand how an OpenFlow-based controller will communicate with an OpenFlow switch in the situation of failovers, discovering new deployments, and such.

Chapter Five
Openflow Packet Details

This chapter describes OpenFlow packet types in detail. The bit and byte level of information is captured per packet. Similar to the other chapters of book, these packets are based on specification 1.0 of OpenFlow standards.

5.1   Summary of OpenFlow Packets

Controller-to-Switch

- Controller-to-switch messages are initiated by the controller and may or may not require a response from the switch.

Asynchronous

- The switch sends these messages to the controller, without the controller triggering these messages from the switch. Switches send asynchronous messages to the controller to denote a packet arrival, switch state change, or error.

Symmetric

- The switch or controller can send these messages to each other without it being triggered from the other end.

5.2 Packets Overview

In the table below is a snapshot of all OpenFlow packets that have been given and classified on the packet type given in specification 1.0. The first column explains the packet type, the second column explains the classification of that packet based on specification, and the third column gives the type value of that particular type of packet in OpenFlow header. Further groupings of packets have been done based on the functionality these packets achieve.

OpenFlow Packet Type	Classification of Packet	Type Value in OF Generic Header
Symmetric Messages		
OpenFlow hello	Symmetric message	0
OpenFlow error	Symmetric message	1
OpenFlow echo request	Symmetric Message	2
OpenFlow echo reply	Symmetric message	3
OpenFlow vendor message	Symmetric message	4
Switch Configuration Messages		
OpenFlow feature request	Controller-to-switch message	5
OpenFlow Feature reply	Controller-to-switch message	6
OpenFlow get configuration request	Controller-to-switch message	7
OpenFlow get configuration reply	Controller-to-switch message	8
OpenFlow set configuration	Controller-to-switch Message	9
Asynchronous Messages		
OpenFlow packet-in	Asynchronous message	10
OpenFlow flow removed	Asynchronous message	11
OpenFlow port status	Asynchronous message	12
Controller command Messages		
OpenFlow packet-out	Controller-to-switch message	13

OpenFlow flow modification	Controller-to-switch message	14
OpenFlow port modification	Controller-to-switch message	15
Statistics Messages		
OpenFlow stats request	Controller-to-switch message	16
OpenFlow stats reply	Controller-to-switch message	17
Barrier Messages		
OpenFlow barrier request	Controller-to-switch message	18
OpenFlow barrier reply	Controller-to-switch message	19
Queue Configuration Messages		
Queue get configuration request	Controller-to-switch message	20
Queue get configuration reply	Controller-to-switch message	21

Table 5.1

5.3   Packet Details

This section details each packet type. The packets are drawn in pictorial format, and each field of packet has been explained in detail.

5.3.1 Generic Protocol Header Format

This packet is generic for all OpenFlow packets and is prepended (every OpenFlow packet will have this packet as outer most header) in all OpenFlow packets. The pictorial format of this generic header is given in Packet 5.3.1.

Packet 5.3.1

```
0                   1                   2                   3                   4
0 1 2 3 4 5 6 7 8 9 0 1 2 3 4 5 6 7 8 9 0 1 2 3 4 5 6 7 8 9 0 1 2
+-+-+-+-+-+-+-+-+-+-+-+-+-+-+-+-+-+-+-+-+-+-+-+-+-+-+-+-+-+-+-+-+
| Version       | Type          |         Message Length         |
+-+-+-+-+-+-+-+-+-+-+-+-+-+-+-+-+-+-+-+-+-+-+-+-+-+-+-+-+-+-+-+-+
|                         Transaction ID                        |
+-+-+-+-+-+-+-+-+-+-+-+-+-+-+-+-+-+-+-+-+-+-+-+-+-+-+-+-+-+-+-+-+
```

Version. This field provides the version of OpenFlow protocol. With OpenFlow specification 1.0, the current value is (ox1).

Type. This field provides the type value of the packet that is being transported in a particular OpenFlow header. Different type values for different packet types are explained in Section 5.2. Below is the snapshot for the type value per packet type.

Type value in OpenFlow header	OpenFlow Packet Type
0	Hello
1	Error
2	Echo Request
3	Echo Reply
4	Vendor
5	Features Request
6	Features Reply
7	Get Configuration Request
8	Get Configuration Reply
9	Set Configuration
10	Packet Input Notification
11	Flow Removed Notification
12	Port Status Notification
13	Packet Output
14	Flow Modification
15	Port Modification
16	Stats Request
17	Stats Reply
18	Barrier Request
19	Barrier Reply
20	Queue Get configuration request
21	Queue get Configuration Reply

Table 5.2

Message length. This field is for representing the total length of the OpenFlow packet that is encapsulated in a particular generic OpenFlow header. The length of the total packet (header + payloads) is represented in octets.

Transaction ID. This field of transaction ID is used to pair the request and reply. The transaction ID of a Reply in a packet will have to match as of the Request packet's transaction ID, to make the pairing clear.

5.3.2 Hello Packet

The hello packet has no specific body in it, it only consists of an OpenFlow header with a type value as 0. Receiver and sender segregate these packets by looking at the type field of the OpenFlow packet header.

5.3.3 Error Packet

Following is the pictorial presentation of an error packet. It is encapsulated in a generic OpenFlow header and sent when certain error situations happen.

Packet 5.3.3

Type value. The type value field in the error packet can have a value from zero to five, and for each type value there could be several code types.

- "Type Value = 0"
  - Reason: hello protocol failed

    When a hello message fails, the error packet with type value equal to zero is sent. It can have the following code values.

Code	Description
0	No Compatible version
1	Permission Error

Table 5.3

- "Type Value = 1"
  - Reason: request not understood

  When an OpenFlow request is not understood, the error packet with type value equal to one is sent. It can have the following code values.

Code	Description
0	Version not supported
1	Header Type not supported
2	Type of Statistics request not supported
3	Vendor not supported
4	Vendor subtype not supported
5	Permission Error
6	Wrong request length for type
7	Specified Buffer is used already
8	Specified buffer does not exist.

Table 5.4

- "Type Value = 2"
  - Reason: error in action description

  When there is an error in the action-descriptor message, the error packet with type value equal to two is sent. It can have the following code values.

Code	Description
0	Unknown Action type
1	Length problem in actions
2	Unknown Vendor ID specified
3	Unknown action type for Vendor ID.
4	Problem Validating output actions
5	Bad action arguments
6	Permission Error
7	Can't handle too many actions
8	Problem Validating output queue

Table 5.5

- "Type Value = 3"
  - o Reason: problem in modifying flow entry

  When an action to modify a flow entry fails, the error packet with type value equal to three is sent. It can have the following code values.

Code	Description
0	Flow not added because of full tables
1	Attempted to add overlapping flow with CHECK_OVERLAP flag set.
2	Permission Error
3	Flow not added because of non-zero idle/ time out.
4	Unknown command
5	Unsupported action list - cannot support in the specified order.

Table 5.6

- "Type Value = 4"
  - o Reason: port modification request failed

  When there is an error in the request for modification of a port, the error packet with type value equal to four is sent. It can have the following code values.

Code	Description
0	Specified port does not exists
1	Specified HW address is wrong.

Table 5.7

- "Type Value = 5"
  - o Reason: queue operation failed

  When there is an error in queue operation, the error packet with type value equal to five is sent. It can have the following code values.

Code	Description
0	Invalid Port
1	Queue does not exists
2	Permission Error

Table 5.8

Data. Interpreted based on the type and code values explained in the above section, this is of variable length. Usually it contains at least sixty-four bytes of the failed request.

5.3.4   Echo-Request Packet

An echo-request packet is just an OpenFlow header plus a data payload for offset. The data offset may have the time stamp to check latency, and it can be of various lengths to determine the bandwidth between the controller and switch. It is recognized by its type value in OpenFlow header.

5.3.5 Echo-Reply Packet

An echo-reply packet is just an OpenFlow header plus a data payload for offset. The data offset may have the same data as the echo request. It is recognized by its type value in OpenFlow header. This packet is sent in reply to the echo-request packet.

5.3.6 Vendor Packet

This packet is to determine vendor uniqueness. If a switch does not understand a vendor ID payload, it should reply with an error packet. Following is the pictorial presentation of a vendor packet.

Packet 5.3.6

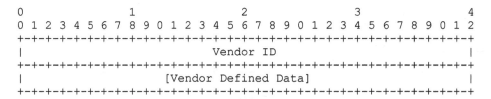

Vendor ID. This is thirty-two–bit data to uniquely identify a vendor. If the OpenFlow switch does not understand the vendor ID, then it should send an error message with "Type = 1, Code = 3."

Vendor-defined data. Vendor-defined data is implementation specific.

5.3.7 Features Request

A feature-request packet is an OpenFlow header plus a data payload for offset. Upon session establishment between the controller and switch, the controller sends the feature-request message to the switch.

5.3.8 Features Reply

A feature-reply message is sent in response to a feature-request message. Upon receipt of the feature request, the switch must respond with the feature-reply message with "specified payload." Typically in a feature request, the controller polls the switch for details on ports available and their details, etc. The switch replies with ports available and their details. Following is the pictorial presentation of a feature-reply packet.

```
                            Packet 5.3.8
0                   1                   2                   3                   4
0 1 2 3 4 5 6 7 8 9 0 1 2 3 4 5 6 7 8 9 0 1 2 3 4 5 6 7 8 9 0 1 2
+-+-+-+-+-+-+-+-+-+-+-+-+-+-+-+-+-+-+-+-+-+-+-+-+-+-+-+-+-+-+-+-+
|                                                               |
+                         Data path ID                          +
|                                                               |
+-+-+-+-+-+-+-+-+-+-+-+-+-+-+-+-+-+-+-+-+-+-+-+-+-+-+-+-+-+-+-+-+
|              Available Number of Packets Can Be Held          |
+-+-+-+-+-+-+-+-+-+-+-+-+-+-+-+-+-+-+-+-+-+-+-+-+-+-+-+-+-+-+-+-+
| # of FlowTabs |                   Padding                     |
+-+-+-+-+-+-+-+-+-+-+-+-+-+-+-+-+-+-+-+-+-+-+-+-+-+-+-+-+-+-+-+-+
|                    Switch Capability Flags                    |
+-+-+-+-+-+-+-+-+-+-+-+-+-+-+-+-+-+-+-+-+-+-+-+-+-+-+-+-+-+-+-+-+
|                    Action Capability Flags                    |
+-+-+-+-+-+-+-+-+-+-+-+-+-+-+-+-+-+-+-+-+-+-+-+-+-+-+-+-+-+-+-+-+
|                     [Port Descriptors]                        |
+-+-+-+-+-+-+-+-+-+-+-+-+-+-+-+-+-+-+-+-+-+-+-+-+-+-+-+-+-+-+-+-+
```

Data path ID. Data path ID is basically a switch ID. This is used for data path identification. The lower forty-eight bits are the switch MAC address, and top sixteen bits are implementation specific.

Available number of packets that can be held. This gives the number of buffered packets that are supported by a data path (for example, the switch).

Number of flow tables. The number of tables supported by a data path (OpenFlow switch) can be between zero to 254. Each table can have its own supported wild-card bits and number of entries. The controller can choose to probe more details on each table size by using a table-type stats request.

Padding. This is for padding.

Switch capability flags. Flags in this packet descriptor give the information on what is supported on the switch. Following is the pictorial presentation of a packet descriptor.

```
                Packet 5.3.8 (i) (Switch Capability flags)
0                   1                   2                   3                   4
0 1 2 3 4 5 6 7 8 9 0 1 2 3 4 5 6 7 8 9 0 1 2 3 4 5 6 7 8 9 0 1 2
+-+-+-+-+-+-+-+-+-+-+-+-+-+-+-+-+-+-+-+-+-+-+-+-+-+-+-+-+-+-+-+-+
|                      Padding                   |H|G|F|E|D|C|B|A|
+-+-+-+-+-+-+-+-+-+-+-+-+-+-+-+-+-+-+-+-+-+-+-+-+-+-+-+-+-+-+-+-+
```

Bit	Description
A	Flow statistics support.
B	Table statistics support.
C	Port statistics support.
D	IEEE 802.1D spanning tree support.
E	Reserved (Must be 0)
F	IP fragmentation support
G	Queue statistics support
H	Matching of IP address in ARP packets

Table 5.9

Action capability flags. This tells in detail which actions are supported by the switch. Following is the pictorial presentation of the packet descriptor of action capabilities flags.

```
         Packet 5.3.8 (ii)  (Action Capability flags)
0                   1                   2                   3                   4
0 1 2 3 4 5 6 7 8 9 0 1 2 3 4 5 6 7 8 9 0 1 2 3 4 5 6 7 8 9 0 1 2
+-+-+-+-+-+-+-+-+-+-+-+-+-+-+-+-+-+-+-+-+-+-+-+-+-+-+-+-+-+-+-+-+
|                         Unused          |M|L|K|J|I|H|G|F|E|D|C|B|A|
+-+-+-+-+-+-+-+-+-+-+-+-+-+-+-+-+-+-+-+-+-+-+-+-+-+-+-+-+-+-+-+-+
```

Bit	Actions associated with flow table or Packets.
A	set Output to switch port
B	Set 802.1Q VID
C	Set 802.1Q PCP
D	Strip 802.1Q tag
E	Set Ethernet source address
F	Set Ethernet destination address
G	Set IPv4 source address
H	Set IPv4 destination address
I	Set IPv4 DSCP
J	Set TCP/UDP source port
K	Set TCP/UDP destination port
L	Output to queue
M	Vendor

Table 5.10

5.3.8.d1 Port Descriptors

Following is the pictorial presentation of a port descriptor packet.

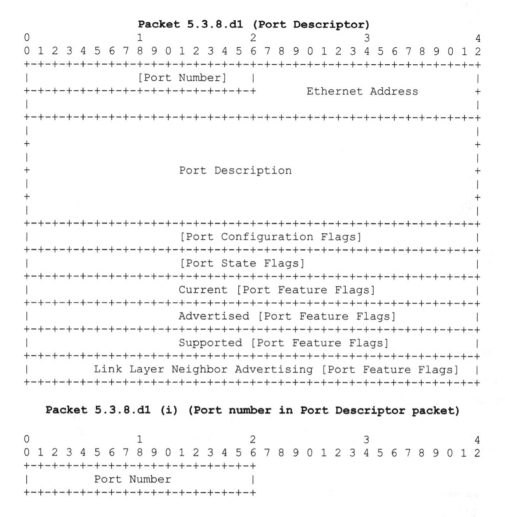

Packet 5.3.8.d1 (Port Descriptor)

Packet 5.3.8.d1 (i) (Port number in Port Descriptor packet)

Port number. Port 0x0000–0xff00 indicates switch ports (port number starts with one). If the port number is within this range, then it specifies a certain port. If the port does not belong in the range 0x0000 to 0xff00, it could have a specific meaning. These ports are called virtual or fake ports.

Below is the table explaining different type of port numbers.

Range	Description	Port Set
0x0000	Reserved	Reserved
0x0001 - 0xff00	Switch ports	Actual port number
0xfff8	Send the packet back on the port where it is received.	In-Port
0xfff9	Perform actions in flow table, only for PACKET_OUT message.	Table
0xfffa	Process the packet using the traditional L2/L3 switching.	Normal
0xfffb	Flood the packet except incoming port.	Flood
0xfffc	Send the packet out all ports except ingress and on STP disabled ports.	All
0xfffd	Send the packet to the controller.	Controller
0xfffe	Send the packet to all switch local OpenFlow ports.	Local
0xffff	Not a physical port in switch.	None

Table 5.11

Ethernet address. This is the MAC address of the port.

Port description. This is the human readable name for the port.

Port-configuration flags. This describes the STP and administrator status on a particular port. The following variables are used to describe the port configuration in the port-descriptor packet and are also used in port-modification message to configure the ports by controller. Controllers can manage these bits, which are used to safely control the network when flooding the packet on the network.

```
Packet 5.3.8.d1 (ii)  (Port Config flags in Port Descriptor packet)
0                   1                   2                   3                   4
0 1 2 3 4 5 6 7 8 9 0 1 2 3 4 5 6 7 8 9 0 1 2 3 4 5 6 7 8 9 0 1 2
+-+-+-+-+-+-+-+-+-+-+-+-+-+-+-+-+-+-+-+-+-+-+-+-+-+-+-+-+-+-+-+-+
|                                                 |P|N|N|N|B|N|A|
|                      Unused                     |I|F|F|B|P|S|D|
|                                                 |N|D|L|P|D|T|M|
+-+-+-+-+-+-+-+-+-+-+-+-+-+-+-+-+-+-+-+-+-+-+-+-+-+-+-+-+-+-+-+-+
```

ADM (Administrator Status): This indicates whether or not a port is administrator down or not

NST (No_STP): Indicates whether the STP is enabled or not; controller may set this bit to one or zero to disable or enable the STP on that port

BPD (Receive BPDU ONLY): This bit can be configured to drop all packets (except BPDU) received on the port

NBP (No Receive BPDU): This bit can be configured to drop any BPDU received on the port

NFL (No Flood): When STP is enabled on port (e.g., NST = 0), STP takes care of this bit on the port; if STP is disabled (i.e. NST = 1), then bit is set to zero

NFD (No Forward): STP running on ports determines if the port will be in forwarding state or not

PIN: Indicates not to send packet-in messages for port

Unused: Must be zero

Port state flags. These bits tell the current state of a port. These bits are not configurable by the controller and are read only.

```
Packet 5.3.8.d1 (iii)  (Port status flag in Port Descriptor packet)
 0                   1                   2                   3                   4
 0 1 2 3 4 5 6 7 8 9 0 1 2 3 4 5 6 7 8 9 0 1 2 3 4 5 6 7 8 9 0 1 2
+-+-+-+-+-+-+-+-+-+-+-+-+-+-+-+-+-+-+-+-+-+-+-+-+-+-+-+-+-+-+-+-+
|                                       |S|S|L|L|       |L|
|                  Mask                 |B|F|R|S| Unused |N|
|                                       |L|W|N|T|       |K|
+-+-+-+-+-+-+-+-+-+-+-+-+-+-+-+-+-+-+-+-+-+-+-+-+-+-+-+-+-+-+-+-+
```

- **LNK (Link state)**
  - Specifies if the link is physically down
- **LST (Listening)**
  - Port is in listening state
- **LRN (Learning)**
  - Port is in learning state
- **SFW (STP-forwarding state)**
  - Traffic is forwarding on the port
- **SBL (STP-blocking state)**
  - Port is not part of STP
- **Mask**
  - Mask to determine the STP state

Port feature flags. The current, advertised, supported, and peer flags in port descriptor are sent in this format.

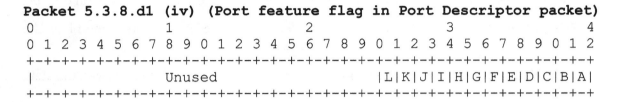

```
Packet 5.3.8.d1 (iv) (Port feature flag in Port Descriptor packet)
0                   1                   2                   3                   4
0 1 2 3 4 5 6 7 8 9 0 1 2 3 4 5 6 7 8 9 0 1 2 3 4 5 6 7 8 9 0 1 2
+-+-+-+-+-+-+-+-+-+-+-+-+-+-+-+-+-+-+-+-+-+-+-+-+-+-+-+-+-+-+-+-+
|                  Unused                   |L|K|J|I|H|G|F|E|D|C|B|A|
+-+-+-+-+-+-+-+-+-+-+-+-+-+-+-+-+-+-+-+-+-+-+-+-+-+-+-+-+-+-+-+-+
```

The details of the bits are as shown in Table 5.12.

Bits	Description
A	10 Mbps Half Duplex
B	10 Mbps Full Duplex
C	100 Mbps Half Duplex
D	100 Mbps Full Duplex
E	1 Gbps Half Duplex
F	1 Gbps Full Duplex
G	10 Gbps Full Duplex
H	Copper medium
I	Fiber Medium
J	Auto Negotiation
K	Pause
L	Asymmetric pause

Table 5.12

5.3.9 Get-Configuration Request

A get-configuration request packet is just an OpenFlow header. This packet is sent by the controller to get the configuration from the switch

5.3.10 Get-Configuration Reply

The switch sends this packet to the controller, explaining the status of the switch configuration. Following is the pictorial presentation of the packet.

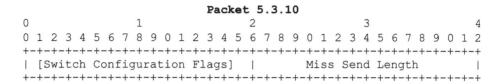

```
                         Packet 5.3.10
0                   1                   2                   3                   4
0 1 2 3 4 5 6 7 8 9 0 1 2 3 4 5 6 7 8 9 0 1 2 3 4 5 6 7 8 9 0 1 2
+-+-+-+-+-+-+-+-+-+-+-+-+-+-+-+-+-+-+-+-+-+-+-+-+-+-+-+-+-+-+-+-+
| [Switch Configuration Flags]  |       Miss Send Length        |
+-+-+-+-+-+-+-+-+-+-+-+-+-+-+-+-+-+-+-+-+-+-+-+-+-+-+-+-+-+-+-+-+
```

Switch-configuration flags.

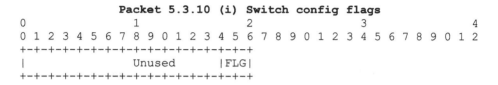

```
                Packet 5.3.10 (i)  Switch config flags
0                   1                   2                   3                   4
0 1 2 3 4 5 6 7 8 9 0 1 2 3 4 5 6 7 8 9 0 1 2 3 4 5 6 7 8 9 0 1 2
+-+-+-+-+-+-+-+-+-+-+-+-+-+-+-+-+
|            Unused         |FLG|
+-+-+-+-+-+-+-+-+-+-+-+-+-+-+-+-+
```

FLG	Action
0	NO Fragmentation handling
1	Drop Fragmented packets
2	Reassemble IP fragments (only if switch capability flag supports)

Table 5.13

Miss send length. This is the maximum octets of new flow that should be sent to the controller. Default value is 128.

5.3.11 Set Configuration

This packet is sent by the controller to the switch for setting the specific status of the post configuration. Packet details are the same as in get-configuration reply. If the controller has to change the configuration it received by get-configuration reply, it will send the same packet with different switch-configuration flags or miss send length (miss send length defines the packet size that a OpenFlow switch can send to controller—only in the case of no flow matched—by default the value is 128 bytes) to set the new configuration.

5.3.12 Packet-In

For all packets that do not have a matching flow entry, or if a packet matches an entry with a send-to-controller action, a packet-in event is sent to the controller. If the switch has sufficient memory to buffer packets that are sent to the controller, the packet-in events contain some fraction of the packet header (by default 128 bytes) and a buffer ID to be used by the controller when it is ready for the switch to forward the packet. Switches that do not support internal buffering (or have run out of internal buffering) must send the full packet to the controller as part of the event. Here is the pictorial presentation of packet-in packet.

Packet 5.3.12

```
 0                   1                   2                   3                   4
 0 1 2 3 4 5 6 7 8 9 0 1 2 3 4 5 6 7 8 9 0 1 2 3 4 5 6 7 8 9 0 1 2
+-+-+-+-+-+-+-+-+-+-+-+-+-+-+-+-+-+-+-+-+-+-+-+-+-+-+-+-+-+-+-+-+
|                        Packet Buffer ID                       |
+-+-+-+-+-+-+-+-+-+-+-+-+-+-+-+-+-+-+-+-+-+-+-+-+-+-+-+-+-+-+-+-+
|     Ethernet Frame Length      |    Ingress [Port Number]     |
+-+-+-+-+-+-+-+-+-+-+-+-+-+-+-+-+-+-+-+-+-+-+-+-+-+-+-+-+-+-+-+-+
|    Reason      |     Padding   |                              |
+-+-+-+-+-+-+-+-+-+-+-+-+-+-+-+-+        Ethernet Frame         +
|                                                               |
~                                                               ~
|                                                               |
+-+-+-+-+-+-+-+-+-+-+-+-+-+-+-+-+-+-+-+-+-+-+-+-+-+-+-+-+-+-+-+-+
```

Packet buffer ID. Identification number for the packet buffered in the switch

Ethernet frame length. Length of the full packet

Ingress port number. Port that receives the packet

Reason. 0: No matching flow; 1: Action explicitly output to controller

Padding. *Padding, if needed*

Ethernet frame. Part of packet (if packet can be buffered) or full packet if it cannot be buffered

5.3.13 Flow-Removed Notification

This packet is sent (in some cases) when the flow is removed from the switch. To understand it in detail, we need to see how the flows are installed. When a flow entry is added to the switch by a flow-modify message, an idle time-out value indicates when the entry should be removed due to a lack of activity, as well as a hard time-out value that indicates when the entry should be removed, regardless of activity.

The flow modify message also specifies whether the switch should send a flow-removed message to the controller when the flow expires (see Section 5.3.16 if bit R is set).

This packet is sent if the flow is deleted for whatever reason, and the R-bit was set when the flow was installed.

Following is the pictorial presentation of this packet.

Packet 5.3.13

```
0                   1                   2                   3                   4
0 1 2 3 4 5 6 7 8 9 0 1 2 3 4 5 6 7 8 9 0 1 2 3 4 5 6 7 8 9 0 1 2
+-+-+-+-+-+-+-+-+-+-+-+-+-+-+-+-+-+-+-+-+-+-+-+-+-+-+-+-+-+-+-+-+
|                                                               |
~                   [Flow Match Descriptor]                     ~
+-+-+-+-+-+-+-+-+-+-+-+-+-+-+-+-+-+-+-+-+-+-+-+-+-+-+-+-+-+-+-+-+
|                                                               |
+                          Cookies                              |
|                                                               |
+-+-+-+-+-+-+-+-+-+-+-+-+-+-+-+-+-+-+-+-+-+-+-+-+-+-+-+-+-+-+-+-+
|           Priority          |     Reason    |    Padding       |
+-+-+-+-+-+-+-+-+-+-+-+-+-+-+-+-+-+-+-+-+-+-+-+-+-+-+-+-+-+-+-+-+
|                Lifetime Duration (seconds)                    |
+-+-+-+-+-+-+-+-+-+-+-+-+-+-+-+-+-+-+-+-+-+-+-+-+-+-+-+-+-+-+-+-+
|              Lifetime Duration (nano seconds)                 |
+-+-+-+-+-+-+-+-+-+-+-+-+-+-+-+-+-+-+-+-+-+-+-+-+-+-+-+-+-+-+-+-+
|          Soft timeout         |          Padding              |
+-+-+-+-+-+-+-+-+-+-+-+-+-+-+-+-+-+-+-+-+-+-+-+-+-+-+-+-+-+-+-+-+
|                                                               |
+               Number of Packets Transferred                  +
|                                                               |
+-+-+-+-+-+-+-+-+-+-+-+-+-+-+-+-+-+-+-+-+-+-+-+-+-+-+-+-+-+-+-+-+
|                                                               |
+                Number of Bytes Transferred                   +
|                                                               |
+-+-+-+-+-+-+-+-+-+-+-+-+-+-+-+-+-+-+-+-+-+-+-+-+-+-+-+-+-+-+-+-+
```

5.3.13.d1 Flow match descriptor packet details

Packet 5.3.13.d1 (Flow match descriptor)

```
0                   1                   2                   3                   4
0 1 2 3 4 5 6 7 8 9 0 1 2 3 4 5 6 7 8 9 0 1 2 3 4 5 6 7 8 9 0 1 2
+-+-+-+-+-+-+-+-+-+-+-+-+-+-+-+-+-+-+-+-+-+-+-+-+-+-+-+-+-+-+-+-+
|                      [Flow Wildcard]                          |
+-+-+-+-+-+-+-+-+-+-+-+-+-+-+-+-+-+-+-+-+-+-+-+-+-+-+-+-+-+-+-+-+
|   Ingress [Port Number]        |                              |
+-+-+-+-+-+-+-+-+-+-+-+-+-+-+-+-+    Ethernet Source Address     |
|                                                               |
+-+-+-+-+-+-+-+-+-+-+-+-+-+-+-+-+-+-+-+-+-+-+-+-+-+-+-+-+-+-+-+-+
|                                                               |
+ Ethernet Destination Address  +-+-+-+-+-+-+-+-+-+-+-+-+-+-+-+-+
|                               |            802.1Q VID          |
+-+-+-+-+-+-+-+-+-+-+-+-+-+-+-+-+-+-+-+-+-+-+-+-+-+-+-+-+-+-+-+-+
|     PCP       |   Padding     |       Ethernet Type           |
+-+-+-+-+-+-+-+-+-+-+-+-+-+-+-+-+-+-+-+-+-+-+-+-+-+-+-+-+-+-+-+-+
| TOS/DHCP      |   Protocol    |          Padding              |
+-+-+-+-+-+-+-+-+-+-+-+-+-+-+-+-+-+-+-+-+-+-+-+-+-+-+-+-+-+-+-+-+
|                   IPv4 Source Address                         |
+-+-+-+-+-+-+-+-+-+-+-+-+-+-+-+-+-+-+-+-+-+-+-+-+-+-+-+-+-+-+-+-+
|                 IPv4 Destination Address                      |
+-+-+-+-+-+-+-+-+-+-+-+-+-+-+-+-+-+-+-+-+-+-+-+-+-+-+-+-+-+-+-+-+
|        Source Port            |       Destination Port        |
+-+-+-+-+-+-+-+-+-+-+-+-+-+-+-+-+-+-+-+-+-+-+-+-+-+-+-+-+-+-+-+-+
```

Flow Wild Card

```
      Packet 5.3.13.d1 (i)(Flow wildcard in Flow match descriptor)
0                   1                   2                   3                   4
0 1 2 3 4 5 6 7 8 9 0 1 2 3 4 5 6 7 8 9 0 1 2 3 4 5 6 7 8 9 0 1 2
+-+-+-+-+-+-+-+-+-+-+-+-+-+-+-+-+-+-+-+-+-+-+-+-+-+-+-+-+-+-+-+-+
|               | | | IPv4 Dst  | IPv4 Src  | | | | | | | | |
| Unused        |J|I|  Address  | Address   |H|G|F|E|D|C|B|A|
|               | | |WildcardMsk|WildcardMsk| | | | | | | | |
+-+-+-+-+-+-+-+-+-+-+-+-+-+-+-+-+-+-+-+-+-+-+-+-+-+-+-+-+-+-+-+-+
```

Details of Bits:

Bits	Description
A	Siwtch Input port
B	Vlan ID
C	Layer-2 Sourse address
D	Layer-2 destination address
E	Ethernet frame type
F	IP Protocol
G	TCP/UDP Source Port
H	TCP/UDP Destination Port
I	Vlan Priority
J	ToS/DHCP

Table 5.14

- **Unused**
    - Must be zero
- **IPv4 Destination Address Wild-Card Mask**
    - IPv4 destination address wild-card bit count. Zero is exact match, one ignores the LSB of IPv4 address, two ignores the two least significant bits…thirty-two and higher, wild card the entire field. This is opposite of the usual convention where /24 indicates that eight bits to ignore.

        Example: Value = 0 Means: 255.255.255.255 1.1.1.1/32 (exact match)

        Value = 8 Means: 255.255.255.0 1.1.1.1/24 (first three octet match)

- **IPv4 Source Address Wild-Card Mask**
    - Same logic as above explained

If no wild cards are set, then the flow-match descriptor exactly describes a flow by using all twelve tuples of the flow table; if all wild cards are set regardless of value of fields, then every flow will match.

- **Ingress Port Number**
  - Port that receives the packet
- **Ethernet Source Address**
  - Layer-2 source address of the flow
- **Ethernet Destination Address**
  - Layer-2 destination address of the flow
- **802.1Q VID**
  - IEEE 802.1Q VLAN identifier; 0xffff means no IEEE 802.1q tag exists
- **802.1Q PRI**
  - IEEE 802.1Q priority
- **Ethernet Type/Length**
  - Ether type of the frame
- **IPv4 Protocol**
  - IPv4 protocol type or ARP type when Ethernet type is 0x0806
- **IPv4 Source Address**
  - IPv4 source address
- **IPv4 Destination Address**
  - IPv4 destination address
- **TCP/UDP Source Port**
  - Layer-4 source port or ICMP type when IPv4 protocol type is 1
- **TCP/UDP Destination Port**
  - Layer-4 destination port or ICMP code when IPv4 protocol type is 1

Flow-match descriptor packet details are over at this point.

Cookies: An identifier issued by the controller.

Priority: For flow-removed packet, this field is for information purposes only (it does not play any role in the flow-removed event). However, in normal flow table, the higher the value of priority, the higher the priority of the flow.

Reason:

- 0 Flow idle time-out exceeded soft time-out.
- 1 Time exceeded hard time-out.
- 2 Evicted by a DELETE flow mod.

Padding: Padding to thirty-two bits.

Lifetime Duration (second): The duration (in seconds) of how long flow is alive in the switch.

Lifetime Duration (nanosecond): The duration (in nanoseconds) of how long flow is alive in the switch.

Soft Time-Out: The soft time-out from original flow mod.

Padding: Padding to sixty-four bits.

Number of Packets Transferred: Number of packets that have hit the flow entry.

Number of Bytes Transferred: Number of bytes that have hit the flow entry.

5.3.14 Port-Status Notification

The switch is expected to send port-status messages to the controller as port configuration state changes. These events include change in port status (for example, if it was brought down directly by a user) or a change in port status as specified by 802.1D. Below is the pictorial presentation of this packet.

```
                          Packet 5.3.14
0                   1                   2                   3                   4
0 1 2 3 4 5 6 7 8 9 0 1 2 3 4 5 6 7 8 9 0 1 2 3 4 5 6 7 8 9 0 1 2
+-+-+-+-+-+-+-+-+-+-+-+-+-+-+-+-+-+-+-+-+-+-+-+-+-+-+-+-+-+-+-+-+
|    Reason     |                                               |
+-+-+-+-+-+-+-+-+                Padding                        +
|                                                               |
+-+-+-+-+-+-+-+-+-+-+-+-+-+-+-+-+-+-+-+-+-+-+-+-+-+-+-+-+-+-+-+-+
|                                                               |
~                    [Port Descriptor]                          ~
|                                                               |
+-+-+-+-+-+-+-+-+-+-+-+-+-+-+-+-+-+-+-+-+-+-+-+-+-+-+-+-+-+-+-+-+
```

Reason

- 0: Port added
- 1: Port deleted
- 2: Port edited

Padding

- Padding to sixty-four bits

Port Descriptor

- Explained in section 5.3.8.d1

5.3.15 Packet Output

When the controller wants to send out any packet to the switch, it triggers a packet-out event, and the packet is sent to the switch. The trigger of this could be the reply of the controller <-> switch messages, or some explicit messages sent by the controller. Below is the pictorial presentation of this packet.

```
                            Packet 5.3.15
 0                   1                   2                   3                   4
 0 1 2 3 4 5 6 7 8 9 0 1 2 3 4 5 6 7 8 9 0 1 2 3 4 5 6 7 8 9 0 1 2
+-+-+-+-+-+-+-+-+-+-+-+-+-+-+-+-+-+-+-+-+-+-+-+-+-+-+-+-+-+-+-+-+
|                        Packet Buffer ID                       |
+-+-+-+-+-+-+-+-+-+-+-+-+-+-+-+-+-+-+-+-+-+-+-+-+-+-+-+-+-+-+-+-+
|   Ingress [Port Number]      | Length of Action Descriptors  |
+-+-+-+-+-+-+-+-+-+-+-+-+-+-+-+-+-+-+-+-+-+-+-+-+-+-+-+-+-+-+-+-+
|                       [Action Descriptors]                   |
+-+-+-+-+-+-+-+-+-+-+-+-+-+-+-+-+-+-+-+-+-+-+-+-+-+-+-+-+-+-+-+-+
|                        [Packet Data]                         |
+-+-+-+-+-+-+-+-+-+-+-+-+-+-+-+-+-+-+-+-+-+-+-+-+-+-+-+-+-+-+-+-+
```

Packet Buffer ID

- Identification number of the packet that is buffered in the switch

Ingress Port Number

- Ingress port number

Length of Actions

- Total length of action list

Action Descriptors

- Refer to Section 5.3.15.d1

Packet Data

- The actual packet the switch needs to send out

5.3.15.d1 Action Descriptor

There are different types of actions that can be taken. Following is a list of actions that can be defined in action descriptor.

Output to Switch Port:

```
           Packet 5.3.15.d1 (i)  (Type 0 in Action Descriptor)
 0                   1                   2                   3            4
 0 1 2 3 4 5 6 7 8 9 0 1 2 3 4 5 6 7 8 9 0 1 2 3 4 5 6 7 8 9 0 1 2
 +-+-+-+-+-+-+-+-+-+-+-+-+-+-+-+-+-+-+-+-+-+-+-+-+-+-+-+-+-+-+-+-+
 |              Type              |              Length             |
 +-+-+-+-+-+-+-+-+-+-+-+-+-+-+-+-+-+-+-+-+-+-+-+-+-+-+-+-+-+-+-+-+
 |        Egress Port Number      |           Max Length            |
 +-+-+-+-+-+-+-+-+-+-+-+-+-+-+-+-+-+-+-+-+-+-+-+-+-+-+-+-+-+-+-+-+
```

- Type = 0
    - Action: Output to the switch port
- Length = 8
- Egress port number: The port number where the packet needs to go out (Refer to Table 3.1.)
- Max Length: The maximum length that can be sent to controller

Set 802.1Q VID:

```
           Packet 5.3.15.d1 (ii)  (Type 1 in Action Descriptor)
 0                   1                   2                   3            4
 0 1 2 3 4 5 6 7 8 9 0 1 2 3 4 5 6 7 8 9 0 1 2 3 4 5 6 7 8 9 0 1 2
 +-+-+-+-+-+-+-+-+-+-+-+-+-+-+-+-+-+-+-+-+-+-+-+-+-+-+-+-+-+-+-+-+
 |              Type              |              Length             |
 +-+-+-+-+-+-+-+-+-+-+-+-+-+-+-+-+-+-+-+-+-+-+-+-+-+-+-+-+-+-+-+-+
 |            802.1Q VID          |            Reserved             |
 +-+-+-+-+-+-+-+-+-+-+-+-+-+-+-+-+-+-+-+-+-+-+-+-+-+-+-+-+-+-+-+-+
```

- Type = 1
    - Action: Set IEEE 802.1Q VLAN
- Length = 8
- 802.1Q VID = IEEE 802.1Q VLAN Identifier

Set 802.1Q PCP:

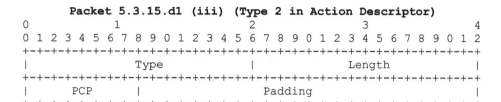

```
         Packet 5.3.15.d1 (iii) (Type 2 in Action Descriptor)
 0                   1                   2                   3          4
 0 1 2 3 4 5 6 7 8 9 0 1 2 3 4 5 6 7 8 9 0 1 2 3 4 5 6 7 8 9 0 1 2
+-+-+-+-+-+-+-+-+-+-+-+-+-+-+-+-+-+-+-+-+-+-+-+-+-+-+-+-+-+-+-+-+
|               Type            |              Length             |
+-+-+-+-+-+-+-+-+-+-+-+-+-+-+-+-+-+-+-+-+-+-+-+-+-+-+-+-+-+-+-+-+
|     PCP       |                 Padding                        |
+-+-+-+-+-+-+-+-+-+-+-+-+-+-+-+-+-+-+-+-+-+-+-+-+-+-+-+-+-+-+-+-+
```

- Type = 2
    o Action: Set IEEE 802.1Q PCP
- Length = 8
- PCP = IEEE 802.1Q PCP (priority)

Strip 802.1Q Tag:

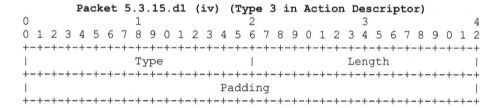

```
         Packet 5.3.15.d1 (iv) (Type 3 in Action Descriptor)
 0                   1                   2                   3          4
 0 1 2 3 4 5 6 7 8 9 0 1 2 3 4 5 6 7 8 9 0 1 2 3 4 5 6 7 8 9 0 1 2
+-+-+-+-+-+-+-+-+-+-+-+-+-+-+-+-+-+-+-+-+-+-+-+-+-+-+-+-+-+-+-+-+
|               Type            |              Length             |
+-+-+-+-+-+-+-+-+-+-+-+-+-+-+-+-+-+-+-+-+-+-+-+-+-+-+-+-+-+-+-+-+
|                          Padding                               |
+-+-+-+-+-+-+-+-+-+-+-+-+-+-+-+-+-+-+-+-+-+-+-+-+-+-+-+-+-+-+-+-+
```

- Type = 3
    o Action: Strip the VLAN tag
- Length = 8

Set Ethernet Address:

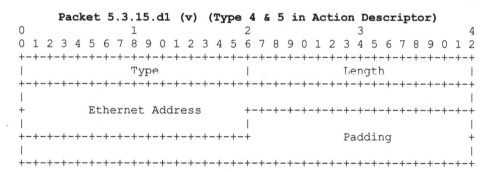

```
         Packet 5.3.15.d1 (v) (Type 4 & 5 in Action Descriptor)
 0                   1                   2                   3          4
 0 1 2 3 4 5 6 7 8 9 0 1 2 3 4 5 6 7 8 9 0 1 2 3 4 5 6 7 8 9 0 1 2
+-+-+-+-+-+-+-+-+-+-+-+-+-+-+-+-+-+-+-+-+-+-+-+-+-+-+-+-+-+-+-+-+
|               Type            |              Length             |
+-+-+-+-+-+-+-+-+-+-+-+-+-+-+-+-+-+-+-+-+-+-+-+-+-+-+-+-+-+-+-+-+
|                               |                                 |
+        Ethernet Address       +-+-+-+-+-+-+-+-+-+-+-+-+-+-+-+-+
|                               |                                 |
+-+-+-+-+-+-+-+-+-+-+-+-+-+-+-+-+            Padding              +
|                                                                 |
+-+-+-+-+-+-+-+-+-+-+-+-+-+-+-+-+-+-+-+-+-+-+-+-+-+-+-+-+-+-+-+-+
```

- Type = 4 and 5
    - Action: Set the source Ethernet address (Type 4); set the destination Ethernet address (Type 5)
- Length = 16
- Ethernet address = the Ethernet address that needs to be set

Set IPv4 Address:

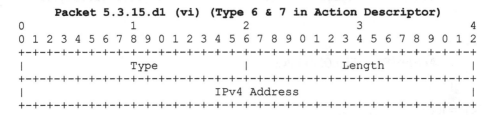

- Type = 6 or 7
    - Action: Set IPv4 source address (for Type 6); Action: Set IPv4 destination address (for Type 7)
- Length = 8

Set IPv4 DSCP:

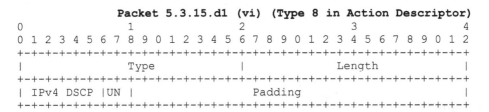

- Type = 8
    - Action: Set the value for IPv4 DSCP
- Length = 8
- IPv4 DSCP = IPv4 DSCP value to be set
- UN = Unused

Set TCP/UDP Ports:

```
        Packet 5.3.15.d1 (vii) (Type 9 & 10 in Action Descriptor)
0                   1                   2                   3                   4
0 1 2 3 4 5 6 7 8 9 0 1 2 3 4 5 6 7 8 9 0 1 2 3 4 5 6 7 8 9 0 1 2
+-+-+-+-+-+-+-+-+-+-+-+-+-+-+-+-+-+-+-+-+-+-+-+-+-+-+-+-+-+-+-+-+
|            Type               |             Length            |
+-+-+-+-+-+-+-+-+-+-+-+-+-+-+-+-+-+-+-+-+-+-+-+-+-+-+-+-+-+-+-+-+
|          UDP/TCP Port         |            Padding            |
+-+-+-+-+-+-+-+-+-+-+-+-+-+-+-+-+-+-+-+-+-+-+-+-+-+-+-+-+-+-+-+-+
```

- Type = 9 and 10
    - Action: Set TCP/UDP source port (Type 9); Action: Set UDP/TCP destination port (Type 10)
- Length = 8

Enqueuing the Packet on a Particular Queue on a Port:

```
        Packet 5.3.15.d1 (viii) (Type 11 in Action Descriptor)
0                   1                   2                   3                   4
0 1 2 3 4 5 6 7 8 9 0 1 2 3 4 5 6 7 8 9 0 1 2 3 4 5 6 7 8 9 0 1 2
+-+-+-+-+-+-+-+-+-+-+-+-+-+-+-+-+-+-+-+-+-+-+-+-+-+-+-+-+-+-+-+-+
|            Type               |             Length            |
+-+-+-+-+-+-+-+-+-+-+-+-+-+-+-+-+-+-+-+-+-+-+-+-+-+-+-+-+-+-+-+-+
|         Port number           |            Padding            |
+-+-+-+-+-+-+-+-+-+-+-+-+-+-+-+-+                                +
|                                                               |
+-+-+-+-+-+-+-+-+-+-+-+-+-+-+-+-+-+-+-+-+-+-+-+-+-+-+-+-+-+-+-+-+
|                           Queue ID                            |
+-+-+-+-+-+-+-+-+-+-+-+-+-+-+-+-+-+-+-+-+-+-+-+-+-+-+-+-+-+-+-+-+
```

- Type = 11
    - Action: Enqueue the packet on a particular port on a given queue
- Length = 16
- Port number: the port on which this queue belongs (Refer to Table 3.1); the value here can be only the physical port or the ingress port
- Queue ID—the queue ID on which the packets need to be enqueued

5.3.16 Flow Modification

Flow-modification message is sent by the controller to the switch for modifying (adding/editing/deleting) a flow in the switch flow table. Below is the pictorial presentation of this packet.

```
                          Packet 5.3.16
  0                   1                   2                   3                   4
  0 1 2 3 4 5 6 7 8 9 0 1 2 3 4 5 6 7 8 9 0 1 2 3 4 5 6 7 8 9 0 1 2
  +-+-+-+-+-+-+-+-+-+-+-+-+-+-+-+-+-+-+-+-+-+-+-+-+-+-+-+-+-+-+-+-+
  |                                                               |
  ~                    [Flow Match Descriptor]                    ~
  |                                                               |
  +-+-+-+-+-+-+-+-+-+-+-+-+-+-+-+-+-+-+-+-+-+-+-+-+-+-+-+-+-+-+-+-+
  |                                                               |
  +                            Cookie                             +
  |                                                               |
  +-+-+-+-+-+-+-+-+-+-+-+-+-+-+-+-+-+-+-+-+-+-+-+-+-+-+-+-+-+-+-+-+
  |           Command           |          Idle Timeout           |
  +-+-+-+-+-+-+-+-+-+-+-+-+-+-+-+-+-+-+-+-+-+-+-+-+-+-+-+-+-+-+-+-+
  |         Hard Timeout        |            Priority             |
  +-+-+-+-+-+-+-+-+-+-+-+-+-+-+-+-+-+-+-+-+-+-+-+-+-+-+-+-+-+-+-+-+
  |                        Packet Buffer ID                       |
  +-+-+-+-+-+-+-+-+-+-+-+-+-+-+-+-+-+-+-+-+-+-+-+-+-+-+-+-+-+-+-+-+
  |      Egress [Port Number]   |         Unused        |E|O|R|
  +-+-+-+-+-+-+-+-+-+-+-+-+-+-+-+-+-+-+-+-+-+-+-+-+-+-+-+-+-+-+-+-+
  |                       [Action Descriptors]                    |
  +-+-+-+-+-+-+-+-+-+-+-+-+-+-+-+-+-+-+-+-+-+-+-+-+-+-+-+-+-+-+-+-+
```

Flow Match Descriptor:

- See details in the flow match descriptor section5.3.13.d1

Command:

- 0 Add new flow
- 1 Modify all matching flows
- 2 Modify entry strictly matching wild-card flows
- 3 Delete all matching flows
- 4 Delete strictly matched wild cards and priority

Soft Time-Out:

- Idle time-out before a flow is expired (in seconds)

Hard Time-Out:

- Maximum time before a flow is expired (in seconds)

Priority:

- Value range is 0.65535

Packet Buffer ID:

- Identification number of the packet, which is buffered in the switch

Egress Port Number:

- See details in packet-descriptor section (port number)

Bit-E:

- Bit for marking emergency flow

Bit-O:

- Bit for checking overlapping entries first

Bit-R:

- Bit for send flow–removed message when flow expires or is deleted

Action Descriptors:

- See Section 5.3.15.d1

5.3.17 Port Modification

Port modification message is sent by the controller to the switch for modifying configurations on the port. Below is the pictorial presentation of this packet.

```
                              Packet 5.3.17
0                   1                   2                   3                   4
0 1 2 3 4 5 6 7 8 9 0 1 2 3 4 5 6 7 8 9 0 1 2 3 4 5 6 7 8 9 0 1 2
+-+-+-+-+-+-+-+-+-+-+-+-+-+-+-+-+-+-+-+-+-+-+-+-+-+-+-+-+-+-+-+-+
|          Port Number         |                               |
+-+-+-+-+-+-+-+-+-+-+-+-+-+-+-+-+        Ethernet Address        +
|                              |                               |
+-+-+-+-+-+-+-+-+-+-+-+-+-+-+-+-+-+-+-+-+-+-+-+-+-+-+-+-+-+-+-+-+
|                   [Port Configuration Flags]                  |
+-+-+-+-+-+-+-+-+-+-+-+-+-+-+-+-+-+-+-+-+-+-+-+-+-+-+-+-+-+-+-+-+
|                [Port Configuration Flags] Mask                |
+-+-+-+-+-+-+-+-+-+-+-+-+-+-+-+-+-+-+-+-+-+-+-+-+-+-+-+-+-+-+-+-+
|                         Advertisement                         |
+-+-+-+-+-+-+-+-+-+-+-+-+-+-+-+-+-+-+-+-+-+-+-+-+-+-+-+-+-+-+-+-+
|                            Padding                            |
+-+-+-+-+-+-+-+-+-+-+-+-+-+-+-+-+-+-+-+-+-+-+-+-+-+-+-+-+-+-+-+-+
```

Port Number:

- Refer to Table 3.1

Ethernet Address:

- Layer-2 MAC address on the port

Port Configuration Flags:

- Explained in Section 5.3.8.d1 (as port-configuration flags)

Port Configuration Flags Mask:

- Masking for the flags explained in Section 5.3.8.d1.(as port-configuration flags)

Advertisement (Port Feature Flags)

- Explained in Section 5.3.8.d1 (as port-feature flags)

Padding:

- Padding to sixty-four bits

5.3.18 Stats Request

The controller sends this message for finding out the statistics. Below is the pictorial presentation of this packet.

```
                        Packet 5.3.18
0                   1                   2                   3                   4
0 1 2 3 4 5 6 7 8 9 0 1 2 3 4 5 6 7 8 9 0 1 2 3 4 5 6 7 8 9 0 1 2
+-+-+-+-+-+-+-+-+-+-+-+-+-+-+-+-+-+-+-+-+-+-+-+-+-+-+-+-+-+-+-+-+
|               Type              |             Flags            |
+-+-+-+-+-+-+-+-+-+-+-+-+-+-+-+-+-+-+-+-+-+-+-+-+-+-+-+-+-+-+-+-+
|                        Stats Body                             |
+-+-+-+-+-+-+-+-+-+-+-+-+-+-+-+-+-+-+-+-+-+-+-+-+-+-+-+-+-+-+-+-+
```

Type:

- 0 OpenFlow switch description
- 1 Information of individual flow
- 2 Information of aggregated flow
- 3 Statistical information of flow table
- 4 Information of port statistics
- 5 Information on queue statistics
- 65535 vendor extensions

Flags:

- Not used

Stats Body:

- With type = 0 (switch description), the stats body is empty
- With type = 1 (information on individual flow), following information comes in stats body field.
  - Fields to match
  - ID of table to read
  - Require matching entries to include this as an output port
- With type = 2 (information on aggregated flow), following comes in stats body
  - Fields to match
  - ID of table to read
  - Require matching entries to include this as an output port
- With type = 3 (information on flow table), the stats body is empty
- With type = 4 (information on port statistics), following comes in stats body
  - Port number, it can be a single port or a list of ports
- With type = 5 (information on queue statistics), following comes in stats body
  - All ports for which information in required
  - All queues ID

5.3.19 Stats Reply

The switch sends this message to the controller in response to a stats request. Below is the pictorial presentation of this packet.

```
                         Packet 5.3.19
 0                   1                   2                   3                   4
 0 1 2 3 4 5 6 7 8 9 0 1 2 3 4 5 6 7 8 9 0 1 2 3 4 5 6 7 8 9 0 1 2
+-+-+-+-+-+-+-+-+-+-+-+-+-+-+-+-+-+-+-+-+-+-+-+-+-+-+-+-+-+-+-+-+
|              Type              |              Flags              |
+-+-+-+-+-+-+-+-+-+-+-+-+-+-+-+-+-+-+-+-+-+-+-+-+-+-+-+-+-+-+-+-+
|                          Stats Body                            |
+-+-+-+-+-+-+-+-+-+-+-+-+-+-+-+-+-+-+-+-+-+-+-+-+-+-+-+-+-+-+-+-+
```

Type:

- 0: OpenFlow switch description
- 1: Information of individual flow
- 2 Information of aggregated flow

- 3 Statistical information of flow table
- 4 Information of port statistics
- 5 Information on queue statistics
- 65535 vendor extensions

Flags:

- 0x0001 more replies to follow

Stats Body:

- With type = 0 (switch description), following comes in stats body
    - Manufacturer description
    - Hardware description
    - Software description
    - Serial number
    - Human readable description of data path
- With type = 1 (information on individual flow), following comes in stats body"
    - Length of this entry
    - ID of table flow came from
    - Description of fields
    - Time flow has been alive in seconds
    - Time flow has been alive in nanoseconds beyond seconds units
    - Priority of the entry (only meaningful when this is not an exact-match entry)
    - Number of seconds flow is idle before expiration
    - Number of seconds before expiration
    - Opaque controller-issued identifier
    - Number of packets in flow
    - Number of bytes in flow
    - Action descriptor
- With type = 2 (information on aggregated flow), following comes in stats body
    - Number of packets in flows
    - Number of bytes in flow
    - Number of flows
- With type = 3 (information on flow table), following comes in stats body
    - Identifier of table (lower numbered tables are consulted first)
    - Wild cards that are supported by the table

- Maximum number of entries supported
- Number of active entries
- Number of packets looked up in table
- Number of packets that hit table
- With type = 4 (information on port statistics), following comes in stats body
  - Number of received packets
  - Number of transmitted packets
  - Number of received bytes
  - Number of transmitted bytes
  - Number of packets dropped by RX
  - Number of packets dropped by TX
  - Number of receive errors (this is a super-set of more specific receive errors and should be greater than or equal to the sum of all RX error values)
  - Number of transmit errors (this is a super-set of more specific transmit errors and should be greater than or equal to the sum of all TX error values—none currently defined)
  - Number of frame alignment errors
  - Number of packets with RX overrun
  - Number of CRC errors
  - Number of collisions
- With type = 5 (information on queue statistics), following comes in stats body
  - Queue ID
  - Number of transmitted bytes
  - Number of transmitted packets
  - Number of packets dropped due to overrun

5.3.20 Barrier Request

A barrier-request packet is an OpenFlow header plus a data payload for offset. The data offset may be used as per vendor's implementation.

5.3.21 Barrier Reply

A Barrier reply packet is just an OpenFlow header plus a data payload for offset. The data offset may be used as per Vendor's implementation.

5.3.22 Queue Get-Configuration Request

The controller can query the switch for configured queues on a port. The controller sends this message to the switch to know the configured queues on a particular port. Below is the pictorial presentation of this packet.

```
                        Packet 5.3.22
0                   1                   2                   3                   4
0 1 2 3 4 5 6 7 8 9 0 1 2 3 4 5 6 7 8 9 0 1 2 3 4 5 6 7 8 9 0 1 2
+-+-+-+-+-+-+-+-+-+-+-+-+-+-+-+-+-+-+-+-+-+-+-+-+-+-+-+-+-+-+-+-+
|              Port Number          |            Padding         |
+-+-+-+-+-+-+-+-+-+-+-+-+-+-+-+-+-+-+-+-+-+-+-+-+-+-+-+-+-+-+-+-+
```

5.3.23 Queue Get-Configuration Reply

The switch replies with this message including details of configured queues on requested particular port. Below is the pictorial presentation of this packet.

```
                        Packet 5.3.23
0                   1                   2                   3                   4
0 1 2 3 4 5 6 7 8 9 0 1 2 3 4 5 6 7 8 9 0 1 2 3 4 5 6 7 8 9 0 1 2
+-+-+-+-+-+-+-+-+-+-+-+-+-+-+-+-+-+-+-+-+-+-+-+-+-+-+-+-+-+-+-+-+
|              Port Number          |            Padding         |
+-+-+-+-+-+-+-+-+-+-+-+-+-+-+-+-+-+-+-+-+-+-+-+-+-+-+-+-+-+-+-+-+
|                        Queuing information                     |
+-+-+-+-+-+-+-+-+-+-+-+-+-+-+-+-+-+-+-+-+-+-+-+-+-+-+-+-+-+-+-+-+
```

Port number. This will be the port number for which the queue configuration is replied. The port numbers are expressed in certain ways (refer to Table 3.1 for details).

Queuing information. This is represented by the following parameters:

- **Queue ID**
  - The ID for the queue. There can be multiple queue IDs for which the information can be given. For each queue ID, the queuing information will have separate variables (tied to that queue ID).
  - For each queue ID, there will be the following variables:
    - Length of the queuing information for that queue ID
    - Property
      - Value = Null; if the value is null, the queuing information for that queue ID terminates here.
      - Value = Minimum Rate limit; if this flag is set, then the queuing information also set the variable which specifies the minimum rate for that queue ID.

Chapter Six
Introduction to VxLAN

This chapter is dedicated to SDN implementation and focused on virtual machines, thus, the technology revolves around solving the issues that arise with virtual-machine evolution. This technology mainly assumes the switches/router-based network abstracted from the server's view. Unlike OpenFlow (which is programmability of switches), this technology is focused on making end-to-end communications between VMs that are separated by network boundaries. The main reasons to focus on this technology were:

► Server virtualization has led to presence of a huge number of virtual machines (VMs) active in the network, which is causing the existing network infrastructure to find a solution to the increase in demand.

► Data centers are growing by the minute as a result of the need to segregate the VMs into groups. This has been traditionally done using the VLANs. However, 4094 VLANs may not be adequate to cater to this increased demand.

► The data centers are hosting multiple tenants, with each tenant's own applications. Each tenant is in its own logical network.

6.1   Challenges with Current Server Virtualization Design

This section explains the specific issues that are becoming exposed with the extensive use of server virtualization.

Limited VLAN Ranges

With data centers increasing in size and capacity, the current virtual LANs (VLAN), which use a twelve-bit VLAN ID, may not be enough to provide necessary broadcast isolation. With this growing demand for virtualization, a need for a solution that is more scalable arises.

Virtual Machine Movement

With virtualization and cloud computing, the VMs can be moved from one server to another seamlessly and with no impact on the VM being moved. However, in the current design, this can only be achieved if the VM is in the same IP subnet. This restriction will not allow VM movement across different IP subnets, and this can be a major issue as the data centers grow in size and complexity. (Please refer Figure 6.1, which depicts the problem with VMotion across different subnets).

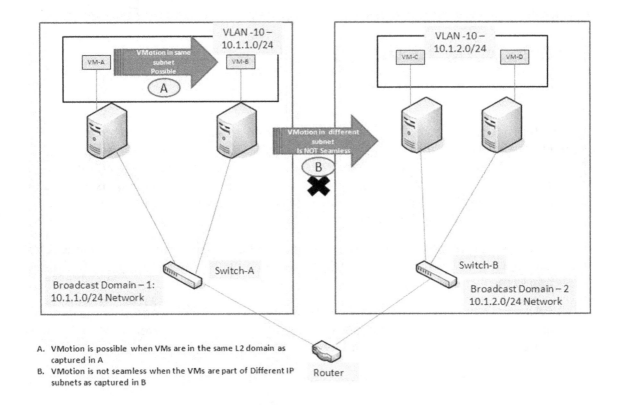

A. VMotion is possible when VMs are in the same L2 domain as captured in A
B. VMotion is not seamless when the VMs are part of Different IP subnets as captured in B

Figure 6.1

Address Table at Top of the Rack Switches

With VMs scaling to the limits, the top of the rack switches that usually connect to the servers have to learn an increased number MAC addresses since there is more number of VMs per server. Further, since there are several racks in a data center, each ToR would need to maintain an address table for VMs that need to talk to other VMs in the data center.

Multi-Tenancy

Data centers are hosting multiple tenants. In the cloud, there is a need to provide elastic services to several tenants, where each of the tenants need traffic isolation. The isolation at Layer-2, as provided by VLANs (twelve-bit, 4094), may not be enough. In the case of Layer-3 networks, there may be two customers using the same Layer-3–addressing scheme, and this may require providing isolation in a different way.

6.2   VxLAN Overview

VxLAN (Virtual eXtensible Local Area Network) is the solution for most of the problems stated in section 6.1.

VxLAN runs over the existing infrastructure and provides a way to extend a Layer-2 network over a Layer-3 network. VxLAN can be termed as a Layer-2 overlay scheme over a Layer-3 network. Each overlay is called a VxLAN segment. VMs within the same VxLAN segment can communicate with each other.

In order for VxLAN to work, the following enabling technologies have been introduced

- **VNI (Virtual Network Identifier):**

This is a twenty-four–bit ID. VNI identifies a VxLAN. This gives almost 16M (2^{24}) VxLANs that can be used. VNI encapsulates the inner frame (the frame that originates at the VM). This encapsulation using VNI helps VxLAN to create a tunnel, which overlays a Layer-2 network on top of a Layer-3 network.

- **VTEP (VxLAN Tunnel End Point):**

This tunnel originates at an end point called a VxLAN Tunnel End Point (VTEP). The tunnel extends from one VTEP to another VTEP, and the tunnel is identified by VNI. The VTEP encapsulates/decapsulates the frames received from/to a VM, where the VM does not know anything about the VNI and VxLAN tunnel.

Two VxLAN segments can have the same MAC address, but one segment cannot have a duplicate MAC address.

VM to VM Packet Flow

Consider a VM within a VxLAN overlay network. This VM is unaware of VxLAN. To communicate with a VM on a different host, it sends a MAC frame destined to the target as before. The VTEP on the physical host looks up the VNI to which this VM is associated. It then determines if the destination Mac is on the same segment. If so, an outer header comprising an outer Mac, outer IP address, and VxLAN header (see Figure 1 in Section 5 for frame format) are inserted in front of the original MAC frame. The final packet is transmitted out to the destination. This is the IP address of the remote VTEP connecting the destination VM (represented by the inner MAC destination address).

Implementation-Specific Methodologies for VxLAN

The control plan for VxLAN can be implemented in several ways. A couple of them have been discussed in VxLAN draft.

- **Learning Based on Data Flows:**

  In data-plane learning, the association of VM's MAC to VTEP's IP is discovered via source learning. For unknown destination, broadcast, and multi-cast traffic, multi-cast is used.

- **Central Repository Based:**

  Another way to distribute VM's MAC to VTEP's IP could be a central distribution–based lookup by the Individual VTEP or distribution of the mapping information to the VTEPs by the central directory.

Treatment of Broadcast/Unknown Unicast/Multi-Cast

In the above VM-to-VM packet flow there was a scenario when the source VM does not know the MAC for the destination VM, and it sends an ARP packet, which is sent by the VTEP using a multi-cast mechanism. In order for this multi-cast mechanism to work, there needs to be a mapping between VxLAN VNI and the IP multi-cast group that will be used to send these packets.

This mapping will enable VTEP to provide IGMP membership reports to the upstream switch/router to join/leave the VxLAN-related IP multi-cast group. Based on this structure, the leaf nodes can be pruned if the member is not available on the host for the specific multi-cast group. Protocol Independent Multicast (PIM) sparse mode, PIM dense mode, and PIM bidirectional can be deployed for VxLAN to function.

6.3 Case Study

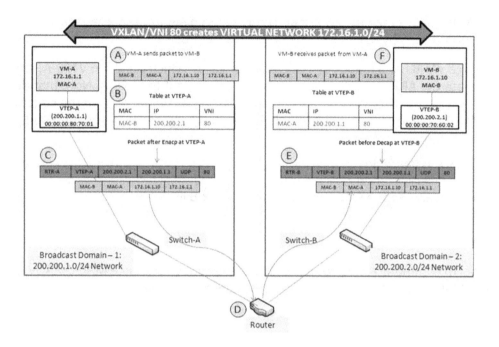

Figure 6.2

This case study explains the functionality of VxLAN, using an example of a deployed network (explained in Figure 6.2). In Figure 6.2, letters represent the steps. Below is the explanation of each step (the starting step is A).

Before the actual VM-to-VM communication happens, there may be a need that ARP between the communicating VMs needs to be resolved. The steps for ARP resolution are given in Step 0.

Step 0

VM-A wants to communicate with VM-B on a different host. It needs to send a frame destined to that VM, however, it does not know the MAC of the destination VM.

    IV. VM-A, which is unaware of VxLAN, sends an ARP packet to learn the MAC address of VM-B.

    V. The ARP is encapsulated in a multi-cast packet by the VTEP-A on the physical server, and this is multi-cast to the group associated with the VNI.

    VI. All the VTEPs associated with that VNI receive the packet and add the mapping VTEP-A/ VM-A MAC to their tables.

VII. VTEP-B also receives this multi-cast packet, it decapsulates the packet, and floods the inner packet, which is the ARP request to all the ports that are part of the VNI for that host.

VIII. VM-B receives the ARP request and constructs an ARP-reply packet and sends to VTEP-B, which is the physical server associated with VM-B.

IX. Since VM-B has a mapping in its table for VM-A, which points to VTEP-A, it will encapsulate the ARP reply into unicast packet and send it to VTEP-A. Note that destination IP will be the IP of VTEP-A. Destination MAC could be the MAC of the next hop router if this is being routed or if it is in the same Layer-2 domain, Destination MAC is MAC of VTEP-A.

X. VTEP-A receives this packet, decapsulates it, and sends the ARP reply to VM-A.

XI. VTEP-A also adds a mapping to its table: VTEP-B IP/VM-B MAC.

Step A

VM-A wants to communicate to VM-B, sends a packet out with source MAC ("MAC-A"), destination MAC ("MAC-B"), source IP 172.16.1.1, and destination IP 172.16.1.10.

Step B

VM-A is unaware of VxLAN, however, the physical server to which VM-A belongs is part of the VxLAN 80. The VTEP end point, VTEP-A in this case, checks the table to confirm if it has an entry for destination MAC-B.

Step C

VTEP-A encapsulates the packet it received from VM-A, adds a VxLAN header with VNI as 80, UDP header with special destination port for VxLAN, new source IP as VTEP-A's IP, new destination IP as VTEP-B's IP, source MAC as VTEP-A's MAC, and destination MAC as the MAC address of the router's interface connecting to the switch A.

Step D

Once this packet reaches the router, it will perform normal routing operation and forward out its interface and modify the source MAC and destination MAC of the outer header.

Step E

The packet reaches the VTEP-B, and since the packet has a UDP header with VxLAN port, VTEP-B decapsulates the packet (everything up to the inner frame is stripped) and sends the inner packet to the destination VM.

Step F

The inner packet is received at the VM-B, which is the correct destination.

6.4   VxLAN Packets

This section explains the packet format for VxLAN encapsulation (the packet is taken from the VxLAN draft).

6.4.1 VxLAN Header

```
                               Packet 6.1
 0                   1                   2                   3                   4
 0 1 2 3 4 5 6 7 8 9 0 1 2 3 4 5 6 7 8 9 0 1 2 3 4 5 6 7 8 9 0 1 2
+-+-+-+-+-+-+-+-+-+-+-+-+-+-+-+-+-+-+-+-+-+-+-+-+-+-+-+-+-+-+-+-+
|R|R|R|R|I|R|R|R|                   Reserved                    |
+-+-+-+-+-+-+-+-+-+-+-+-+-+-+-+-+-+-+-+-+-+-+-+-+-+-+-+-+-+-+-+-+
|      VxLAN Network Identifier (VNI)        |      Reserved     |
+-+-+-+-+-+-+-+-+-+-+-+-+-+-+-+-+-+-+-+-+-+-+-+-+-+-+-+-+-+-+-+-+
```

Flags (8 Bits):

I Flag *must be* set to one for a valid VxLAN network ID (VNI). Remaining seven bits are reserved fields and must be set to zero.

VxLAN Segment ID/VxLAN Network Identifier (VNI):

This is a twenty-four–bit field used for identifying individual VxLAN overlay networks on which communicating VMs are situated. VMs in different overlay networks cannot communicate with each other.

Reserved Fields:

(Twenty-four bits and eight bits)—*Must be* set to zero for padding purposes.

6.4.2 Outer UDP Header

```
                               Packet 6.2
 0                   1                   2                   3                   4
 0 1 2 3 4 5 6 7 8 9 0 1 2 3 4 5 6 7 8 9 0 1 2 3 4 5 6 7 8 9 0 1 2
+-+-+-+-+-+-+-+-+-+-+-+-+-+-+-+-+-+-+-+-+-+-+-+-+-+-+-+-+-+-+-+-+
|        Source Port = xxxx         |     Dest Port = VxLAN Port |
+-+-+-+-+-+-+-+-+-+-+-+-+-+-+-+-+-+-+-+-+-+-+-+-+-+-+-+-+-+-+-+-+
|          UDP Length               |        UDP Checksum        |
+-+-+-+-+-+-+-+-+-+-+-+-+-+-+-+-+-+-+-+-+-+-+-+-+-+-+-+-+-+-+-+-+
```

The outer UDP header with a source port provided by the VTEP and the destination port is a well-known UDP port that is vendor specific. The UDP check sum should be zero. As per VxLAN draft, a packet will be accepted for decapsulation if it comes with UDP check sum equals to zero.

6.4.3 Outer IP Header

```
                              Packet 6.3
0                   1                   2                   3                   4
0 1 2 3 4 5 6 7 8 9 0 1 2 3 4 5 6 7 8 9 0 1 2 3 4 5 6 7 8 9 0 1 2
+-+-+-+-+-+-+-+-+-+-+-+-+-+-+-+-+-+-+-+-+-+-+-+-+-+-+-+-+-+-+-+-+
|Version|  IHL  |Type of Service|         Total Length          |
+-+-+-+-+-+-+-+-+-+-+-+-+-+-+-+-+-+-+-+-+-+-+-+-+-+-+-+-+-+-+-+-+
|  Identification               |Flags|     Fragment Offset     |
+-+-+-+-+-+-+-+-+-+-+-+-+-+-+-+-+-+-+-+-+-+-+-+-+-+-+-+-+-+-+-+-+
|  Time to Live  |    Protocol   |        Header Check sum        |
+-+-+-+-+-+-+-+-+-+-+-+-+-+-+-+-+-+-+-+-+-+-+-+-+-+-+-+-+-+-+-+-+
|                   Outer Source Address (IPv4)                  |
+-+-+-+-+-+-+-+-+-+-+-+-+-+-+-+-+-+-+-+-+-+-+-+-+-+-+-+-+-+-+-+-+
|                   Outer Destination Address                   |
+-+-+-+-+-+-+-+-+-+-+-+-+-+-+-+-+-+-+-+-+-+-+-+-+-+-+-+-+-+-+-+-+
```

The outer IP header contains the source IP/destination IP of the VTEP over which the VM communications are happening. Rest of the IP header follows typical IP header definitions, which can be obtained from the VTEP.

6.4.4 Outer Ethernet Header

```
                              Packet 6.4
0                   1                   2                   3                   4
0 1 2 3 4 5 6 7 8 9 0 1 2 3 4 5 6 7 8 9 0 1 2 3 4 5 6 7 8 9 0 1 2
+-+-+-+-+-+-+-+-+-+-+-+-+-+-+-+-+-+-+-+-+-+-+-+-+-+-+-+-+-+-+-+-+
|                   Outer Destination MAC Address               |
+-+-+-+-+-+-+-+-+-+-+-+-+-+-+-+-+-+-+-+-+-+-+-+-+-+-+-+-+-+-+-+-+
| Outer Destination MAC Address |    Outer Source MAC Address    |
+-+-+-+-+-+-+-+-+-+-+-+-+-+-+-+-+-+-+-+-+-+-+-+-+-+-+-+-+-+-+-+-+
|                    Outer Source MAC Address                    |
+-+-+-+-+-+-+-+-+-+-+-+-+-+-+-+-+-+-+-+-+-+-+-+-+-+-+-+-+-+-+-+-+
Optional Ethertype=C-Tag 802.1Q |  Outer.VLAN Tag Information    |
+-+-+-+-+-+-+-+-+-+-+-+-+-+-+-+-+-+-+-+-+-+-+-+-+-+-+-+-+-+-+-+-+
|       Ethertype 0x0800        |
+-+-+-+-+-+-+-+-+-+-+-+-+-+-+-+-+
```

The outer Ethernet header contains the source MAC of the source VTEP. The outer destination MAC address in this header may be the address of target VTEP or of an intermediate Layer-3 router.

6.4.5 Inner Ethernet Header and Payload

This is the native Ethernet packet coming from the source VM (which needs to be encapsulated by VxLAN).

Bibliography

[1] OpenFlow Specification 1.0.0 : http://www.openflow.org/documents/openflow-spec-v1.0.0.pdf

[2] IPRFC   : www.ietf.org/rfc/rfc791.txt

[3] OSPF RFC   : www.ietf.org/rfc/rfc1583.txt

[4] BGP RFC   : www.ietf.org/rfc/rfc1771.txt

[5] TCP RFC   : www.ietf.org/rfc/rfc793.txt

[6] UDP RFC   : www.ietf.org/rfc/rfc768.txt

[7] OpenFLow Shortest Path   : http://staff.science.uva.nl/~delaat/rp/2011-2012/p25/report.pdf

                                   http://www.dis.uniroma1.it/~demetres/docs/dapsp-full.pdf

[8] Quantum API   : http://openvswitch.org/openstack/2011/07/25/openstack-quan-tum-and-open-vswitch-part-1/

[9] SDN overview   : http://www.networkcomputing.com/data-networking-management/searching-for-an-sdn-definition-what-is/240000171

                                   : https://www.opennetworking.org/

[10] VxLAN Specification   :

[11] VxLAN Packet Flow   : http://www.nvc.co.jp/pdf/product/arista/Arista_Networks_VxLAN_White_Paper.pdf

[12] OpenFlow Packets   : http://www.openflow.org/wk/images/c/c5/Openflow_packet_format.pdf